NEW MEXICO'S
Best

Richard Mahler

Fulcrum Publishing
Golden, Colorado

Maps included in this book are for general reference only. For more detailed maps and additional information, contact the agencies or specific
sites listed.

Library of Congress Cataloging-in-Publication Data

Mahler, Richard.
    New Mexico's best / Richard Mahler.
        p. cm.
    Includes index.
    ISBN 1-55591-232-X (pbk.). — ISBN 1-55591-341-5 (6-copy prepack)
    1. New Mexico—Guidebooks. I. Title.
F794.3.M34   1996
917.8904'53—dc20   96-24148
                                                              CIP

Printed in the United States of America

0   9   8   7   6   5   4   3   2   1

Fulcrum Publishing
350 Indiana Street, Suite 350
Golden, Colorado 80401-5093
(800) 992-2908 • (303) 277-1623

NEW MEXICO'S
Best

Contents

Acknowledgments

The author wishes to express his deep appreciation to the many individuals who contributed suggestions, enthusiasm, research, constructive criticism, and moral support to this project. A partial list includes (in alphabetical order): Debora Bluestone, Valerie Brooker, Merilyn Brown, Grove Burnett, Rita Cadena, Mike Chappell, Mary Lou Cook, Debbie Carley, Sue Dirksen, Kate Droney, David Dunaway, M. L. Duncan, Larry Frank, Vickie Gabin, Dan Gibson, Anne Griffin, Susan Hazen-Hammond, Sukey Hughes, Lucita Hurtado, Jerry Jordan, Katharine Kagel, Jeff Kline, Eric Larson, Lynda Leonard, Jack Loeffler, Alejandro Lopez, Helen Lucero, Charlie Luthin, Sandy McKnight, Don and Mary Mahler, Monty Mickelson, Ann Muriel, Tom and Alise Noble, John Norton, Michael Oellig, Phil Lynch, Gerald Peters, Ken Peterson, Elaine Pinkerton, Mike Pitel, Doug Preston, Kate Priest, Harrison Schmitt, Wolf Schneider, Molly Seymour, Jim Smith, Diana Stephens, Betsy and David Tighe, Claire Tyrpack, Don Usner, Peggy van Hulsteyn, Linda Velarde, Steele Wotkyns, and Lucie Yeaman. There are many other names that should be listed here, but time, space, and memory have conspired against them. Please accept my apologies for any oversight.

Special thanks to Kate Droney, for her excellent navigation on research trips and invaluable editorial assistance. *Muchas gracias* also to the scores of friendly, helpful, and anonymous New Mexicans I met along the way. Without them, this would not be the best state in the union. Finally, much gratitude goes to my editor at Fulcrum, Carmel Huestis, who was excited about this project from the beginning.

Preface

*F*irst, a few words about what this book is *not*.

New Mexico's Best is *not* a standard travel guide that tries to give the reader a detailed, opinionated summary of scenic attractions, hotels, restaurants, and gift shops. There are many fine books about New Mexico that provide this valuable service already and you are encouraged to use them. The author often travels with two or more guidebooks and recommends the practice highly. After all, you wouldn't buy a car or a house without shopping around, so why spend a lot of money on a vacation without soliciting a second (or even a third) opinion?

Now, a few words about what this book *is*.

New Mexico's Best is a specialized guide with two main goals. First, it seeks to get travelers off the beaten path so that they can experience some delightful people, places, and events often missed by other books. Its second goal is to share what New Mexicans themselves like about their state. The author has interviewed hundreds of residents (plus some former residents) and synthesized their expert opinions on what they feel is best about The Land of Enchantment.

This process raises some obvious questions. How does one decide what *is* or *isn't* best about a place? To be sure, one person's dream vacation may be another's nightmare. Who can claim to be a legitimate "expert"? How can one trust someone else's subjective definition of what's "best"?

I have no solid answers … certainly none that would stand up in court. But put simply, the experts in this book are people whom I trust— New Mexicans who know the subject well enough to have what I consider to be an intelligent and informed opinion. In some cases, their expertise may seem obvious. Who better to evaluate the quality of a restaurant than someone who runs or reviews them for a living? In other instances, the connection may seem unclear. But I think a school teacher can legitimately recommend a goat farm to children if he's taken his classes there and gotten to know the owners. And I believe an outdoor-loving biologist is in a good position to judge a hiking trail or campsite. Yet I've also tapped experts who don't necessarily have any direct professional affiliations with a category, but whose point of view is deemed valid simply because I recognize and value their passionate interest in the subject. A speech therapist qualifies as an authority on salsa dancing, in my book, if I believe she deeply and truly loves the merengue, cumbia, and cha-cha-cha.

I looked high and low for these experts, inquiring among family, friends, and strangers. I used conventional sources: tourist brochures, chamber of commerce handouts, guidebooks, publicists, and in-state publications such as regional magazines and newspapers. I visited restaurants, hotels, parks, and other tourist enterprises incognito, not disclosing my identity as a travel writer. Finally, I relied on my own experience as an on-and-off New Mexico resident, reporter, and explorer since the 1950s.

I'll close with an important disclaimer. In the course of my research, I asked specifically that New Mexicans *not* share with me anything that they feared might be spoiled or destroyed by an increase in visitation. If there was any possibility that a place was too fragile, too sacred, too rare, or too special to survive the scrutiny of more tourists, I left it out. I believe strongly that a travel writer must use his or her conscience in determining how the world might be changed by his or her recommendations. If you feel I've made some poor decisions in this regard, please let me hear from you. This book will be updated periodically and your comments will have a direct bearing on what changes are made.

There are bound to be great differences of opinion and I sincerely want to hear from readers who disagree. It is inevitable that listings of what's "best" will change with each update of *New Mexico's Best*. Some entries will become outdated or inappropriate, while new categories will appear. Please send any and all suggestions, corrections, and comments to me in care of Fulcrum Publishing, 350 Indiana Street, Suite 350, Golden, Colorado 80401. With your help, our next edition will be the best yet.

One last reminder! All telephone numbers listed are prefaced by the New Mexico area code—505—unless otherwise indicated. (Note that when dialing long-distance numbers within the state, you must dial the area code first.)

NEW MEXICO'S
Best

Chapter 1

The Best of the Best

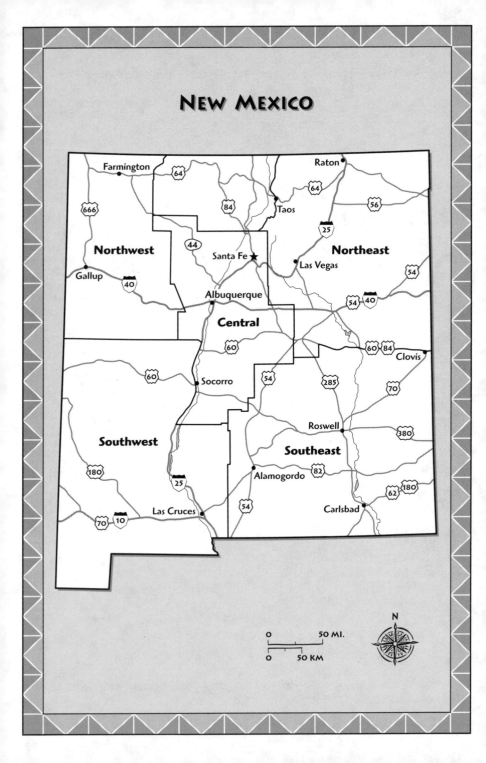

$\mathcal{S}$ome of the best things about the Land of Enchantment don't fit into discrete geographic categories. They pertain instead to New Mexico's distinctive character and resist geographic pigeonholes. Others relate to the region's tri-cultural heritage: Native American, Hispanic, and Anglo (a catch-all category here that includes virtually everyone who doesn't fit the other two classifications). In compiling this chapter, a wide range of "experts" were chosen to reflect on these qualities.

1 What's Best about New Mexico

Rep. Bill Richardson

Bill Richardson was born to U.S.-Mexican parents and grew up in Mexico City. After moving to New Mexico in the late 1970s, Richardson became involved in local Democratic politics. He eventually was elected to Congress, where he continues to represent the northern part of the state and serves as chief deputy whip in the House. Richardson has built an international reputation as a peacemaker—defusing volatile situations in North Korea, Burma, Haiti, Bosnia, Cuba, and Iraq, as well as New Mexico—and has been nominated for the Nobel Peace Prize. Here's Congressman Richardson's perspective on what's best about his adopted home:

"New Mexico, while home to extraordinary museums, art galleries, and restaurants, is more a state of mind, illuminated by contrasts so poignant they capture the interest of all who visit our remarkable state and encounter our warm and friendly people.

"The Land of Enchantment has a fascinating history of three diverse cultures. The rich heritage of the ancient Indian cliff dwellers, the Spanish conquistadors, and the Anglo pioneers are preserved today in wonderful ceremonials, fiestas, fairs, and rodeos; in beautiful arts and crafts; and in delicious foods throughout the state.

"New Mexico is world renowned for advancements in science and technology, but intermingling threads of yesteryear weave an alluring pattern of past and present, old and new. Remnants of historic Route 66 border bustling freeways; ghost towns and frontier forts scatter about computer chip companies and air force bases; and farms, ranches, and dairies surround nuclear research laboratories.

Few states can claim such multifaceted landscapes as can New Mexico. Both metropolitan areas and rural communities alike lay amidst rugged mesas and canyons, rocky deserts, snowcapped mountains, and rolling plains.

These magnificent contrasts represent the best of New Mexico to me."

2 Best Way to See the "Real" New Mexico

Jim Sagel

Jim Sagel has lived in the Española Valley of northern New Mexico since the early 1970s, working as an educator, translator, and writer. An Anglo transplant from Colorado, he taught himself to read, write, and speak Spanish after marrying into the family of local weaver Teresa Archuleta. "I wanted to protect myself from my in-laws," Sagel jokes. "After I'd learned the language, I became fascinated with the stories that my *suegros* [in-laws] were telling. I started writing them down—and creating stories of my own." For more than 20 years now, Sagel has been writing, in both Spanish and English, about the Española Valley. His poems and short stories have won numerous awards—including Cuba's prestigious Premio Casa, the Latin American equivalent of the Pulitzer. In Sagel's opinion, *wandering* is the best way to see the "real" New Mexico:

"From the first time I crossed the New Mexico state line, I decided to wander. There is something about the grandfatherly mountains, the isolated adobe villages, and meandering arroyos that immediately invited me off the map. Now, more than a quarter of a century later, I continue to cruise the back roads of my adopted home, not unlike that first 'lowrider,' Cristóbal Colón, who discovered far more than he was looking for.

"These aimless trips down Frost's 'untaken road' have led me to the most austere and remarkably beautiful landscapes—likewise, they have brought me into contact with the most hospitable and civilized people in this nation, the *nuevo mexicanos* of the small villages and pueblos who truly mean it when they say, '*Mi casa es tu casa*,' even after so many have taken them literally and taken over their land.

"Wandering is what inspired the following selection from my unpublished manuscript of 'road love poems' to New Mexico, *Unexpected Turn:*

"*Pass With Care*, the sign cautions, but you need no reminding as you pass by a butte brooding over stegosaurus hills. You know that the next turn always promises the unexpected, a ponderosa laid open by lightning, a herd of cattle sleek as a Brahman vision, a lake tremulous with trout. This is a land where the sky intoxicates the eye and history gossips in the willows lining the river. It's the lost roads that lead to the desert gardens; you miss your turn and end up finding your way.

"You turn your eyes to the ridge above the pueblo and gaze at the deer dancers descending in the frozen dawn. You turn on the wooden dance floor in your lover's arms, as the *músicos* play the *valses* their grandfathers learned from their grandfathers. You turn a hoe over in the mud to make the adobes for the home you are already plastering in your dreams. You turn your head just long enough for the *abuelo*, the grotesque and guffawing trickster, to steal your hat, leaving you to squint at the *Matachines* dancing their masked ritual. You turn over in your hands the *santo* that has emerged from the root of a cottonwood tree; you trace the water serpent coiled around a pot burnished black as an unbroken memory.

"Once you have known this land, you will always turn back. Like the exiled lover who could sense his lover combing her hair from a thousand miles away, you will always hear the drum pounding in your pulse, the *Llorona* weeping in your inner ear, the sand cranes flapping their wings along side the river in your blood. Once you have taken the unexpected turn, you will never again pass without caring."

<u>3</u> *Best* Way to Appreciate New Mexico's Hispanic Culture

Rudolfo Anaya

If one is to savor New Mexico's best qualities fully, it is good to know something about the people who make this their home. No group is more significant in this regard than *los Hispanos*—the people of mixed Spanish, Native American, and Mexican blood whose ancestors have been here for generations.

Although they make up the largest single ethnic group in New Mexico—an estimated 40 percent of the state's 1.6 million residents in 1996—Hispanos are little understood by many who live in the other 49 states. It's not widely known, for example, that the first Europeans to establish settlements within the present borders of the United States were the Spanish colonists of the upper Río Grande Valley—in 1598—and not the Pilgrims of Plymouth Rock or Jamestown. Another common misconception is that the Spanish-speaking people of today's New Mexico are mostly south-of-the-border immigrants or the descendants of recent immigrants. The reality is that New Mexico's Spanish-language culture is something apart from that found in Mexico, Latin America, Spain, Texas, or California. This is why many of the state's Spanish-speakers bristle when outsiders label them "Mexican," "Chicano," or "Latino." None of these labels really fit, thus the widespread acceptance of the term "Hispano," a usage here that dates back many years.

When I broached the subject with New Mexico's best-known Hispano writer, Rudolfo Anaya told me, "The best way to get a feel for the *Nuevo Mexicano* culture is to get off the beaten path." Anaya, a native of the state's eastern plains and the author of the widely acclaimed novel, *Bless Me Última,* writes more eloquently than I can paraphrase:

"If you're lucky you'll be invited by someone to visit a home. Perhaps a baptism is taking place, or a wedding dance. Maybe the *Matachines* are dancing in Bernalillo, or, if it's December, they'll be dancing at Jémez Pueblo. If someone invites you, go! Nuevo Mexicanos are proud of their history and traditions—they love to show them off.

"The *mayordomo* who invites you into a small village church will share real history with you and the living experience of being New Mexican. The *mayordomo* of an *acequia* will teach you more about water rights and their historical importance than volumes in the library.

"The places of New Mexico, from rugged peaks and green pine forests to the southern Las Cruces desert, are truly magical. We understand why there is 'beauty all around us.' We dream and contemplate the sacred landscape. But for a real sharing of our cultural ways, go to the people. In villages, pueblos, ranches, or in the big *barrios* of the big cities, if you find someone willing to take you by the hand and share: Go!

"One day I was up at my home in Jémez Springs, picking a harvest of golden delicious apples. A German couple came by and asked to buy some of my apples. I not only gave them a bag of apples, I gave them copies of my books. During that brief visit we became good friends. Later I received a letter from them thanking me for the glimpse into my life.

"So, if you find a guide, go! It's the people—*la gente*—who make this a great state."

4 Best Way to Appreciate New Mexico's Native Culture

Simon Ortíz

Simon Ortíz is a native of Ácoma Pueblo, west of Albuquerque, who has lived in urban and rural communities throughout New Mexico, as well as on the Navajo Reservation in Arizona. He is an eloquent, critically-acclaimed poet and short story writer, whose books include *Going for the Rain*, *Woven Stone,* and *After and Before the Lightning.* His work synthesizes his Native American heritage with images from the modern world. Ortíz is also a dynamic teacher, and in the late 1980s he served as the official interpreter/translator for his tribe. Like Rudolfo Anaya, he is much better able to describe his cultural perspective than I am:

"I have always felt a sense of awe when I've been out in the country. Growing up at Ácoma Pueblo and in New Mexico I think there's a natural inspiration—a sense of wonder and respect. There's an awe in seeing something that's beyond oneself and realizing that we are only a small part of whatever that something is. It's recognizing what the land is—stone, trees, soil, cactus— and what is attended to that land—wind, sun, rain, snow.

"I grew up in the Ácoma village of McCartys, and as a child I heard depictions of the way our land was a long time ago. The elders used to talk about when grass came up to a horse's belly. I never saw grass this high. My father said that the grass got shorter, the land became eroded, and the rains no longer came. This happened not long after the federal government wiped out the prairie dogs. But before that they had killed the coyotes and then the prairie dogs proliferated. And because the prairie dogs were supposedly the cause of the erosion, they were also killed. What this tells me is that whenever there's some kind of unnatural disturbance—some break in the ecological system that Mother Nature has provided—things get out of whack.

"We must take responsibility for what is happening today … there must be a belief in continuance and in this there is hope, knowing that the human population of the Southwest can work for something more than survival … Life will go on when we really take care of ourselves and take care of the land. Non-Indian people are coming to share our realization that survival isn't meaningful if it doesn't include tending, seeking, nourishing, and enhancing life. Until we deal with that reality there is no way that the land is going to survive nor are we going to continue with it. We need to be responsible for making the earth a healthy place, a place of beauty.

"We can learn from those who know the value of that way of life, such as Native American people. However, I believe we have to come to a love and respect for ourselves. We have the human spirit in ourselves: love, self-respect, appreciation for each other's qualities, and that capacity to show that to each other for the sake of our own serenity. … Native American elders say when they pray that this knowledge is for all of us—to help Mother Earth and to help us in our continuance upon her."

5 *Best* Way to Behave on an Indian Reservation

Above all, be respectful. Assuming you're not a Native American, come to dances, celebrations, festivals, and ceremonies *only* when they're announced as open to non-Indian visitors. Often these are summer feast days, saints' days, Christian religious holidays, New Year's Day, and King's Day (January 6).

Remember that most structures are private residences. Don't climb on walls or buildings; don't stare into windows and doorways. Don't enter sacred grounds, such as cemeteries or *kivas*. Minimize talking during dances and ceremonies; and don't applaud when they're over. These are religious ceremonies and clapping, whistling, or shouting is inappropriate. (Allowances may be made when dances and other ceremonies are conducted at events catering specifically to non-Indians.) Don't engage in photography, sketching, or tape recording unless specific permission has been granted: inquire first.

If You Go: "Each pueblo operates under its own sovereign government and establishes its own rules for visitors," advises the **Eight Northern Indian Pueblos Council (852-4265),** which gives away an official visitors' guide. The directory lists all pueblo events open to the public during the course of the year.

Insider Tip

At **Santa Fe's Indian Market** and associated events, photography is allowed, but be polite and secure permission first. Ask before touching merchandise and avoid long chats with the artists unless sales are slow. Some sellers will haggle over prices, others won't. In general, the prices of smaller items are fixed. By the end of the second day of Indian Market more artists are willing to bargain their prices down slightly. The market takes place the third weekend of August each year.

6 *Best* New Mexican Food

"Quite simple, chile represents our national identity," declares Paul W. Bosland, a professor of agriculture at New Mexico State University and director of The Chile Institute. "What oranges are to Florida and potatoes are to Idaho, chile is to New Mexico."

Better known as "Dr. Chile," Bosland carries on a scientific research tradition that began at NMSU nearly a century ago. Chile growing is serious business in New Mexico and chile accompanies a wide variety of dishes in New Mexicans' homes and restaurants, including soups, salads, entrées, and even desserts. Most chile, however, is locally consumed in a roasted, chopped, and seasoned form that may be eaten with enchiladas, burritos, rellenos, and other traditional dishes—or served as a side dish.

There are more than 35,000 acres devoted to chile cultivation here, far more than in any other state (although hay is still New Mexico's biggest farm crop). The acreage is increasing, as the state strives to keep up with a seemingly insatiable national demand. In 1993, for example, it was revealed that chile-flavored salsa had surpassed ketchup as America's favorite food condiment.

"Some of the same kinds of chile we eat today have been harvested by Native Americans for at least 10,000 years," says Bosland, a contributing editor of Albuquerque-based *Chile Pepper* magazine. "The Indians of South America, where the pepper originated, have been spicing their food with chile for much longer than that."

In answer to the most commonly heard question in New Mexico—"Do you want red or green?"—Bosland advises that red tends to be milder, if picked at roughly the same time and place. In fact, most green chiles that are left to mature will eventually turn red. The smallest red chiles, however, tend to be much hotter than their green counterparts.

"When in doubt," says Dr. Chile, "order 'Christmas.' That way you'll get a little of each."

Other chile trivia include these factoids:

◆ A rainforest native, the chile plant is a fruit and its peppers are, technically, berries. Chile falls into the same plant family as tomatoes, petunias, tobacco, and deadly nightshade. Some people are allergic to all of these.

◆ Chile is not only rich in Vitamins C and A—richer, by weight, than oranges and carrots—it also releases the body's endorphins, the same powerful natural painkillers responsible for "runner's high." This may explain why some people seem to become addicted, literally, to eating the stuff. Chile also contains beta-carotene, which studies suggest may reduce the risk of cancer.

◆ Habañero chiles, grown only in the subtropics, are 70 times as hot as the jalapeño peppers that macho college students sometimes dare each other to consume. So far, they are the world's hottest known chiles.

◆ Medicinal use of chile as a painkiller dates back centuries, and it has been cultivated as a food since at least 3400 B.C. Chile causes sinus drainage and perspiration, which might offer another benefit. "As we perspire, evaporation on our skin makes us feel cool," says Bosland. "This cooling effect may be why chile is popular in warm climates." Several studies also show that chile helps protect the stomach by increasing mucous flow—and does not harm normal stomachs, lead to ulcers, or retard the healing of ulcer. (Some people are allergic to chile, however, and it does cause heartburn and indigestion in others.)

◆ *Chile* is the correct spelling of the word in New Mexico, used to describe the plant, the pepper pod, and the condiment or soupy sauce made from the pod. *Chili* refers to the chile-with-onions-beans-and-meat stew that is the official state dish of Texas. *Chilli* is a Native American version of the same word.

◆ For further information about New Mexico chiles and the status of the long-anticipated **Chile Museum,** contact the **Chile Institute in Las Cruces** at **646-3028.**

When in Santa Fe, gourmands are strongly advised to check out **The Chile Shop (109 East Water Street)** and **Coyote Café General Store (132 West Water Street)** for the best selection of chile condiments and paraphernalia, including scores of bottled salsas and even Christmas lights shaped like red chile peppers.

Insider Tip During late summer and early fall, you can buy fresh chiles all over New Mexico. They are a familiar sight even in grocery store parking lots, where gas-heated ovens are set up to roast them on the spot. Indeed, many New Mexicans will swear to the benefits of "chile therapy"—among them Danny Rubin, a screenwriter (his movies include *Groundhog Day*) and an instructor at the College of Santa Fe:

"In early fall the green chile pepper harvest comes to town. Now, you wouldn't just buy a pepper and eat it like a southwestern banana, and you can't chop them raw and expect to impress people with your salsa. Chiles gotta be roasted. Every grocery store in town sets up these big fuel-injected hamster cage things in their parking lots during chile season. You buy a half-bushel or so of peppers, and the guy tosses them into the hopper, turns up the flame thrower, and sets the cage a-spinning. Right away you can smell that transcendent smell—a smell right up there with the chimney smoke from burning piñon on a winter's night. In a few minutes your cage stops and the guy dumps a half-bushel of charred, black peppers into a plastic garbage bag, exactly as it's been done for generations. In the bag they steam, and by the time you get home you can set about to pulling the black skins from the now soft, cooked, green pulp. Now you can seed 'em, chop 'em, freeze 'em, or whatever. But before I do anything else, I take some fresh bread, spread on a little mayonnaise, and load it up with a layer of the warm, chopped chile. THAT is a taste you don't get out of a can. And for a few exquisite moments it's just about the best thing in the world next to Charley Parker and sex, both of which can accompany and enhance the experience. Yes, in Santa Fe you can get your crystal-choker homeopathic alignment, or you can do a few weeks of chile therapy. Each has its merits, I am sure."

7 *Best* Way to Pick, Roast, and Eat Piñon Nuts

Piñones—the delicious nuts of the piñon pine tree—are a bonafide New Mexico gourmet treat. Not to be confused with nuts of the stone pines found in Italy, Spain, and China, these nutritious morsels are harvested each fall by hand (mostly by freelance Navajo pickers) throughout the state's high-desert woodlands. They sell retail for about $8 per pound.

Once they are shelled and roasted, piñon nuts make a wonderful addition to salads, sauces, candies, cookies, and pestos, or can be eaten all by themselves. There's a real knack, though, for efficiently picking and preparing the tiny nuts, which have a sweetish flavor and aroma that adds a New Mexican accent to cooking.

"Most experienced pickers use a sheet or blanket," reports Jeff Kline, an environmental education consultant and founding secretary of the New Mexico Piñon Nut Industry Trade Council. "The sheet is placed on the ground underneath a tree that is heavily laden with nuts. Someone shakes the trunk or branches until the piñones fall out of their cones. They are then scooped up and placed in a sack or can."

Kline points out that collecting piñones costs no money and "allows you to meet local people in a noncommercial way." He recommends storing raw nuts in a cool, dry place, then soaking them in water for 10 minutes before roasting them on a cookie sheet at 350° for 15 to 20 minutes.

"Unfortunately," he sighs, "there's no easy way to get them out of their shells. You can use a hammer, rolling pin, or standard nutcracker. Although my dentist wouldn't approve, I think the best way is simply to crack them open with your teeth."

As a reward for this considerable effort, piñones are not only delicious, but nutritionally very rich, providing many essential amino acids and proteins. Their high oil content makes the nuts a wonderful source of energy for hikers and others who exert themselves outdoors.

If You Go: Check with the **State Land Office (827-5760)** for advice on where to pick piñones. The public may trespass on state-owned lands to pick nuts for their own use and the commissioner's office keeps track of where crops are most plentiful. The BLM and U.S. Forest Service don't seem to worry about trespassing piñon nut pickers and the latter gives away pamphlets on how and where to pick piñones. Private property owners should always be consulted before picking on their land: every year there are loud complaints from individuals who resent the small number of inconsiderate pickers who leave litter, tire tracks, and other debris. The thickest concentrations of nut-bearing piñon trees are found mostly between 6,000 and 8,000 feet in elevation. **The Piñon Nut Council** will make recommendations on prime picking spots. It can be reached through the State Land Office at the above number. The best use of piñones in restaurant cooking is found at **La Casa Sena in Santa Fe.**

> **Insider Tip** "The best time to gather piñones is in mid- to late October," says Jeff Kline, "after the first frost opens the cones but before the first snow covers up nuts that have fallen."

Because of a complex set of scientific factors having to do with irregular plant and weather cycles, piñon nut crops vary dramatically from year to year and place to place. A given tract of piñon forest will yield a good crop about once every seven years.

8 Best Time to Visit

Throughout most of New Mexico, particularly at higher elevations and in northern counties, the four seasons are very distinct, marked by weather patterns that change dramatically in the course of a year, yet are almost always sunny.

Summer is fine for those on a traditional vacation schedule and winter makes sense for skiers. Spring is pretty, if also fickle and windy. In Santa Fe and Taos, snow sometimes falls in May, or even June. Many New Mexicans agree that the very best time to visit is late summer and early autumn, particularly that special time from mid-September to mid-October when days are warm and nights are crisp. In the valleys and forests, this is when many trees show their fall colors, and gardens in town are still full of late summer flowers and produce. In parts of the state that suffer the most heat—places like Carlsbad Caverns, White Sands, and Las Cruces—late autumn and winter are perfect times to visit. The months with the fewest visitors—and deepest discounts— are January and February.

If You Go: The **New Mexico Department of Tourism** publishes several visitors' guides and maintains an excellent, toll-free information service. Call **800-545-2040** or **827-7447**. An ongoing source of good material is *New Mexico* magazine, published monthly by the same agency.

Insider Tip Whenever you come, don't forget to look up. "My favorite part of living in New Mexico is the sky," confesses Herbie Mann, a jazz recording artist who spent most of his life in New York. "Oh what a sky! My wife, Janeal Arison, and I never cease to be amazed by the endlessly gorgeous days. It seems that regardless of how terrible the weather may be everywhere else, the sun shines 97 percent of the time in New Mexico."

9 Best New Mexico Kid Stuff

Here's the "totally awesome ten," according to a random selection of New Mexicans under the age of 16. Like check it out, dude.

1. Outdoor sports and nature stuff—Whitewater rafting on the Río Grande (summer), skiing and snowboarding in the mountains (winter), mountain-biking and hiking anywhere (anytime), visiting the Río Grande Zoo and Nature Center (in Albuquerque), collecting cool rocks (Rock Hound State Park), and exploring the old Indian caves at Bandelier National Monument (near Los Alamos) or Puyé Cliffs (Santa Clara Pueblo).

2. Kid-friendly museums—The Children's Museum (Santa Fe), the Museum of International Folk Art (Santa Fe), the Wheelright Museum's summer storytelling by Joe Hayes (Santa Fe), the Museum of Natural History (Albuquerque), the Rattlesnake Museum (Albuquerque's Old Town), the Space Museum (Alamogordo), the Tinkertown Museum (Sandía Park), the Smokey Bear Museum (Capitán), and the International UFO Museum (Roswell).

3. Kid-friendly stores—Jackalope (Bernalillo and Santa Fe), Earth Home (Santa Fe), Albuquerque Rock Gym (Albuquerque), Zuma's Electronic Café (Santa Fe), most pet stores, and any shopping mall (Cottonwood in Albuquerque is the state's biggest).

4. Carlsbad Caverns National Park—Older kids especially like the ranger-led tours of the King's Palace and Slaughter Canyon Cave. There are even more adventurous "wild cave" tours available to teens, including exotic Spider Cave.

5. Railroads—Take a ride on the Toltec & Cumbres Railroad (Chama), Santa Fe Southern (Santa Fe), and Alameda Park Miniature Railway (Alamogordo).

6. Burning of Zozobra—What child can resist the sight of a 50-foot-high, moaning-in-agony puppet named Zozobra (Old Man Gloom) going up in flames, while kids dressed in fairy costumes dance joyfully at its feet and swing sparklers in the night? The burning starts the first night of Santa Fe Fiesta, held the Friday after Labor Day in Ft. Marcy Park.

7. Albuquerque International Balloon Fiesta—This 10-day spectacle in early October features hundreds of soaring hot-air balloons of every shape and size imaginable. It's an event children will happily get out of bed early for.

8. Rodeos—This is the West and everybody should go to a rodeo at least once, especially if he or she loves horses, Brahma bulls, clowns, and cowboys. They are held on weekends in communities throughout New Mexico during summer and fall. Check local newspapers or chambers of commerce for details.

9. The New Mexico State Fair—Scary rides, junk food, arcade games, farm animals, giant pumpkins, cheap trinkets, loud music, and the passing human parade. Need we say more? The state fair is held in Albuquerque for 10 days in mid-September.

10. Cliff's Amusement Park—Cheap thrills that will make kids scream, moms nervous, and dads act 12 years old again. It's in Albuquerque at 4800 Osuna NE (881-9373), and open year round.

Runner-up: The Beach Waterpark, 3 Desert Surf Circle NE (345-6066), which brings surfing and water-sliding to the desert.

10 Best Way to Learn More about New Mexico's Best

Besides this book, there are several regional magazines and newspapers that compile "best of" lists with some regularity. These include *ABQ Magazine, Santa Fean, Santa Fe Reporter, Crosswinds, Alibi* (Albuquerque), and *New Mexican* (Santa Fe). Each provides helpful insights into what local people like to see and do. *New Mexico* magazine's publishing arm also produces first-rate specialized books about the Land of Enchantment, including an annual complimentary *Vacation Guide*. If you don't see it, ask for it.

Chapter 2
Santa Fe and Vicinity

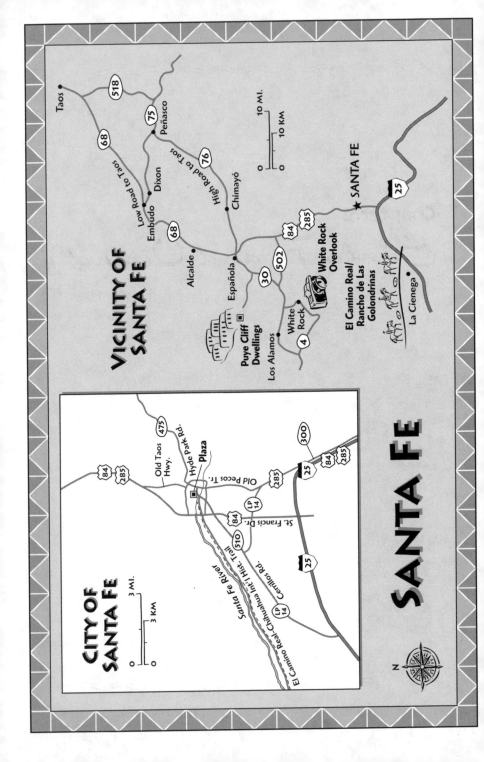

What's Best about Santa Fe

"The moment I saw the brilliant, proud morning sun shine high up over the desert of Santa Fe," wrote British novelist D. H. Lawrence after his first visit to New Mexico's capital, "something stood still in my soul."

First impressions of Santa Fe may no longer be quite so poetic—visitors of the 1920s didn't have to deal with fast-food franchises and summer traffic jams—but the primary attractions of "The City Different" remain unchanged. Santa Fe still sits under an enormous turquoise sky, nestled in a fold between a brown desert plain and lush, green mountains, about 60 miles northeast of Albuquerque. Santa Fe's light is still clear and strong, and the flat-roofed, earth-toned adobes continue to give this place a distinct architectural character.

Some of these charms are wearing a bit thin or have been overlaid with the veneer of modern American commercialism, yet Santa Fe continues to be loved for what she *was* as much as what she *is*. Santa Fe is loved because, as she ages (and the old gal is almost 400), she retains the irrepressible ability to shock, surprise, and, yes, even delight.

My best advice is to avoid Santa Fe during midsummer, when tourists often outnumber the city's 65,000 year-round residents. Unless you're a fan of Native American art, don't come during **Indian Market,** the third weekend of August, when Santa Fe is virtually immobilized by visitors. In general, if you come between Memorial Day and Labor Day, your image of the downtown core may be soured by the large crowds, high prices, lack of parking, and "adobe Disneyland" ambiance you're sure to encounter. Do yourself a favor: come here when things are calmer, slower, and more like they used to be, before Santa Fe was the name of a cookie, a cologne, and a "style."

Don't get me wrong, Santa Fe in summer is still wonderful. If this is when you are able to visit, by all means come! The real magic of Santa Fe transcends the crowds and commercialism. And if you come in summer, take full advantage of the city's marvelous cultural smörgasbord, which groans with delicious offerings from June through August. The best of these include the outdoor opera (north of town), outdoor Shakespeare play (at St. John's College), Santa Fe Chamber Music Festival, Spanish Market, and Santa Fe Stages (a dance/theater series at the College of Santa Fe). Summer is also the best time to shop 'til you drop, dine outdoors, stroll up Canyon Road arm-in-arm with a loved one, climb Cross of the Martyrs Hill to watch the sunset—then sleep the deep, dreamy sleep of the truly contented.

The best time to visit? Early September through the end of October are my favorite weeks in Santa Fe, as locals reclaim their town and get ready for the long winter. (It can snow from late October through early May here, an average of 32 inches each winter.) Indian summer in Santa Fe is a time of warm days and crisp nights. The aspen are gold and the apple trees heavy with their sweet fruit. Children are back in school and the fiestas are over. In fall this feels like a place where people really work and live.

Remember to get lost at least once. Let yourself stumble upon restaurants and shops that aren't in any guidebook. Savor a leisurely meal at a sampling of the many first-class restaurants here. Be sure to take in some of the fine tourist-related attractions—but remember that the *real* Santa Fe, the one D. H. Lawrence fell in love with, is found elsewhere. Look up at a sky filled with thunderheads, or marvel at a sunset. The ever-changing cloudscape, the play of light and shadow, the intensity of color, the air that smells of pine needles and champagne … can still calm the soul as it stirs the spirit.

1 Best (and Worst) Ten Tourist Traps

There's nothing intrinsically wrong with a "tourist trap." In some cases such notoriety is justified, but sometimes not. Based on the author's informal and unscientific survey of Santa Fe residents and visitors, conducted from 1988 to 1996, the ten best (and worst) tourist traps in The City Different include, in no particular order:

The Best

1. Native American art vendors under the Palace of the Governors portal—Both the Indians and the jewelry are genuine. The sellers are friendly, the quality is high, and the prices are fair.

2. Santa Fe Opera—A setting so spectacular and productions so lavish that even people who hate opera love it. The July–August repertoire is wide-ranging, from popular classics to world premieres.

3. Santa Fe Chamber Music Festival—The musicians are first-class, the program is diverse, and the setting—a few steps from the plaza—is marvelous.

A scene from a 1996 production of "Emmeline" at the Santa Fe Opera. Photo courtesy of the Santa Fe Opera.

4. Fiesta's burning of Zozobra (the *first* time)—Probably the biggest community-wide pagan ritual in the United States, but be prepared for a boisterous crowd. It happens the first Friday after Labor Day and is part of the commemoration of the Spanish reconquest of Santa Fe in 1692.

5. Christmas Eve farolitos, luminarias, and caroling—Snow on the ground, piñon smoke in the air, flickering firelight on the adobe walls, and goodwill in the hearts of singing pedestrians. For a few dark hours in December, it feels as if heaven has come to earth and peace will prevail.

6. The Museum of New Mexico—The state of New Mexico maintains four separate, well-curated facilities, each with its own character and charm, and each worthy of an extended visit. Buy a discount ticket and see them all.

7. St. Francis Cathedral and Cristo Rey Church—This is a Roman Catholic city—its name means "Holy Faith"—and religious traditions are still strong. For a glimpse of the beauty of these, take a quiet walk through Santa Fe's biggest churches. Better yet, attend a Sunday mass.

8. Canyon Road Art Walk—On Friday and Saturday nights, particularly during warm months, the city's galleries open their doors and invite the public to experience any and all forms of visual art, from paintings to photographs, from ceramics to sculpture. Its all free—including refreshments.

9. Gardens—You'll notice them everywhere during summer and fall: full of hollyhocks, columbines, lilacs, and cosmos. While you're on the Canyon Road Art Walk, linger for a soothing moment at the carefully tended, multiblossomed **El Zaguán**, dominated by two enormous horse chestnut trees and open daily, 9:00 A.M. to 6:00 P.M.

10. Restaurants—There are more than 150 to choose from, including some of the finest and most celebrated in the United States. Don't be afraid to splurge. After all, you're on vacation!

The Worst

1. The plaza during summer—It's crowded with people. It's encircled by noisy, smelly cars. There's no restroom. It's full of tourists, not locals. Come back during the other nine months, when you'll at least find a place to sit down.

2. Fiesta's burning of Zozobra (*after* the first time)—When you're surrounded by 10,000 people—too many of them drunk and disorderly—you wonder why you didn't stay home, order a pizza, and watch it on cable TV.

3. The "oldest" house—Age is relative and claims are dubious. When this house was being built, hundreds of Native Americans in other parts of New Mexico were dwelling in homes where their descendants have lived to the present day.

4. The "oldest" church—Another case of relativity. **San Miguel Mission** has been around for a long time, but there are contenders for this title in every corner of the world—and other parts of the United States.

5. New Mexico State Capitol Building—You can take a tour of "the Roundhouse" and watch the legislature if you'd like—they convene only during January, February, and sometimes March. But other than the unusual architecture and some interesting public art, there's not much worth seeing.

6. Loretto Chapel—It's small, authentic, and pretty, but not a must-see unless there's a concert—in which case you *should* definitely attend. The so-called "miraculous staircase" is no miracle, although the story is lovely.

7. Indian Market—Take a relatively small, quiet town of 65,000 people. Add 100,000 tourists and hundreds of Native American art vendors. Stir well, block off traffic, and place in a hot sun to bake. Need we say more?

8. Coyote and Kokopelli-themed "art"—Who can explain fashion? The howling coyote and humpbacked flute player (Kokopelli), once wonderful, evocative southwestern images, have been trivialized beyond restoration. Do the planet a favor: don't buy any.

9. Restaurants—Speaking of coyotes, the **Coyote Café** is a place no self-respecting coyote would be caught dead. The food is pretty good—although it's often spiked with too much chile—but the noise level is deafening and the prices astronomical. You can do better. Other overrated destinations—according to many folks in the know—include **María's, La Posada,** and **Rancho de Chimayó.** Ask around before making those "big splurge" reservations.

10. The La Fonda Hotel lobby—This is the famous "inn at the end of the Santa Fe Trail." For decades, the world walked through its front door. But the world—and Santa Fe—has changed. You'll detect a faint echo of what once was, but the characters and conversations that once made the La Fonda lobby special will never return.

2 *Best* Guided Tour

Whether you walk or ride, a guided tour is a great introduction to The City Different and helps ease congestion on narrow, downtown streets. Monty Mickelson, Santa Fe-based travel writer, novelist, and occasional tour guide, believes **Loretto Line** offers the best motorized tours. Based at the Inn at Loretto, the company's daily tours provide a thorough inspection of major attractions in an open-air trolley driven by a well-informed guide.

For those who have more of an interest in history, Mickelson recommends the **Museum of New Mexico**'s daily tours, guided by historian-trained museum docents stationed at the **Palace of the Governors**. While you're waiting for your motorized or on-foot tour to start, take time to view the impressive collection of artifacts in the palace, constructed in 1610 and the oldest government building in the United States.

If You Go: **Loretto Line Tours (983-3701)** begin at the corner of Old Santa Fe Trail and Alameda every hour between 10:00 A.M. and 3:00 P.M. during summer (less often during other months). **Palace of the Governors–based tours (827-6480)** are offered daily from 10:00 A.M. to 5:00 P.M. Both cost about $10 per person.

3 *Best* Museum

There is no place on earth quite like Santa Fe's **Museum of International Folk Art.** Yes, there are other folk art museums in the United States, but none as exuberant, good-humored, and diverse as this. The cornerstone Girard Collection is a real gem: a fantastic and fanciful array of more than 100,000 objects gathered and carefully curated for display by Alexander Girard, an architectural designer whose work took him all over the world.

What makes this collection unique, besides its seemingly endless and eclectic variety, is the way in which Girard—who died in 1993—grouped his objects into a harmonious whole. He could see beyond the differences in an assortment of dolls and masks, for example, and find their cross-cultural commonalty. This is a showcase for the human spirit, as expressed by untrained artists near and far. That's one reason Girard insisted that the items not be labeled, so that they could be experienced with unmitigated awe and wonder. (For those with a need to know, a printed guide provides detailed descriptions of each piece.)

Besides the Girard Wing, which never changes, other noteworthy sections of the museum include a comprehensive multimedia display documenting New Mexico's rich Spanish colonial history.

"If you want to know what New Mexico is all about, the 'Familia y Fé' exhibit is a 'must-see,'" says Stanley Marcus, the co-founder of the famous Nieman Marcus department store, who has homes in both Dallas and Santa Fe.

Marcus—author of *Quest for the Best*, a book about his worldwide search for high-quality merchandise—calls the Folk Art "the Smiling Museum," because "people always come out smiling. I've never seen that happen at any other museum."

If You Go: The **Museum of International Folk Art (827-6350)** is at **707 Camino Lejo,** 3 miles east of the plaza (buses run about every half hour). It is part of a three-museum complex that includes the state-owned **Museum of Indian Arts and Culture** and the privately-owned **Wheelwright Museum of the American Indian.** Each is open daily from 10:00 A.M. to 5:00 P.M. except for Mondays in January and February, or on major holidays. There are no restaurants. Admission is $2, or $5.25 for a three-day pass to all of the Museum of New Mexico's Santa Fe units. (Sunday is "dollar day" for New Mexico residents.)

Insider Tip If your timing is right, folk artists and musicians will be on hand to show and explain how their traditions are continuing into the twenty-first century. You may also see demonstrations of Indian pottery making, weaving, beadwork, or other Native American craftwork at the Museum of Indian Arts and Culture, just across the parking lot from the Folk Art. In the opposite direction, the Wheelwright Museum has similar demonstrations as well as a full-scale, working reproduction of a reservation trading post.

4 *Best* Train Ride

Actor Michael Gross is widely recognized as the aging hippie dad on NBC-TV's *Family Ties*, but he's best known among railroad preservationists as the man who saved the Santa Fe. The part-time area resident was horrified to learn four years ago that the Atchison, Topeka & Santa Fe planned to abandon all service to Santa Fe and remove tracks laid down in 1879. Gross and his business partners bought and improved the line, built a bike path along its right-of-way, and restored passenger service for the first time since 1960.

The one (and only) engine of the Santa Fe Southern Railway.

"I didn't want to see this thing vanish," declared Gross, a lifelong railroad aficionado whose grandfather was an AT&SF switchman in Iowa.

The **Santa Fe Southern** now hauls people and freight—from beer to volcanic cinders—on several round-trips each week to Lamy, a junction 18 miles east that connects with the main line to Chicago and Los Angeles. Kids of all ages are welcome to climb aboard one of the venerable passenger coaches or old-fashioned cabooses that Gross collects and restores.

The *Southern* comprises only one engine and a handful of cars, but a wealth of information is dispensed in transit by railroad buffs who often serve as conductors and firemen.

You'll rumble through roadless woodlands, with fine views of the Sangre de Cristo Mountains, then wind down a steep escarpment into the Galisteo Basin. There's a 90-minute layover in Lamy, where you can eat your picnic lunch and explore this historic village. The century-old **Legal Tender**—where President Rutherford B. Hayes and Billy the Kid once dined—is open for lunch, dinner, and drinks.

Be forewarned that this is a s-l-o-w ride (top speed is around 20 miles per hour). Sodas are sold en route and riders may bring their own food. Best viewing is from the two seats perched in the caboose's cupola.

If You Go: The **Santa Fe Southern** (**989-8600**) departs the Guadalupe Street Depot at 10:30 A.M. every Tuesday, Thursday and Saturday, returning about 3:00 P.M. Round-trip fare is $21 for adults, $16 for 7- to 13-year-olds and those over 60, $5 for children 3 to 6, and free for toddlers. From May 10 through September, a Friday train leaves at sunset and returns about 10:30 P.M. The $30 fare includes dinner, drinks, and entertainment.

5 *Best* Place for Kids

The hands-on **Santa Fe Children's Museum** "offers kids a chance to learn by doing," says local writer (and parent) Catherine Coggan, author of *Family Adventures in New Mexico.* "There's a climbing wall, bubble-making machine, a contraption containing 180,000 metal pins, magnet exhibits, as well as snakes and other live animals that children can touch or hold." Other highlights include a kind of human gyroscope, modeled on a device used by the astronauts to simulate weightlessness, and a pair of outdoor parabolic reflectors that throw voices over long distances. Special science and art classes are offered periodically, as well as puppet shows and concerts.

Coggan names **Jackalope** a runner-up in this category. The "folk art by the truckload" emporium has a prairie dog village, petting zoo, ice cream stand, and periodic fun events that include a Mexican jumping bean race and pumpkin-carving festival. A South American macaw named Salsa lives in the greenhouse and the main store is full of amazing toys and knickknacks—from African masks to Yugoslavian zithers. Ethnic craftspersons are often on hand to show how they create their work and there's live music on weekends.

If You Go: Suited to visitors 12 and under, the **Santa Fe Children's Museum** (**989-8359**) is at **1050 Old Pecos Trail** and open 10:00 A.M. to 5:00 P.M. Thursday through Saturday, and noon to 5:00 P.M. on Sunday. Admission is $2.50 for adults, $1.50 for kids under 12. Free for everyone the first Sunday of the month. **Jackalope** (**471-8539**) is at **2820 Cerrillos Road,** open from 9:00 A.M. to 7:00 P.M. daily. There's a second location on Hwy 44 in Bernalillo, about 15 miles north of Albuquerque.

Insider Tip Adults may want to make a side trip within the Children's Museum building to visit the **Bataan Memorial Museum (474-1670),** which displays some of the 30,000 items commemorating the large number of New Mexican soldiers involved in World War II's infamous Bataan Death March. Open 7:30 A.M. to 4:30 P.M. daily except Sunday; admission is free.

6 *Best* Spa

In 1992, **Ten Thousand Waves** was voted "the best place to send friends" in a poll conducted by the *Santa Fe Reporter* newspaper. In other years, readers have often dubbed it "the best place for a romantic first date." Whatever the "best of" category, locals can't seem to get enough of this elegant Japanese-style *onsen* (outdoor health spa). Tourists, too, can enjoy that special pampered feeling that comes from indulging in a deep tissue massage, steamy sauna, or soothing chlorine-free outdoor hot tub—there are eight private tubs and one communal tub. Sixty therapists are on call, specializing in such exotica as *watsu* (underwater) massages and steamy herbal wraps.

"They sure don't have this in Passaic!" exclaimed one New Jersey visitor. And there's nothing else like Ten Thousand Waves in Santa Fe, either. Efficient, yet relaxed; close to the plaza, yet enclosed by a cozy canopy of piñon pines, this is a restorative refuge for mind, body, and spirit. Prices are not cheap—you can run up a three-figure bill in an eye blink—but your soul will thank you for it. For true decadence, rent one of the exclusive guest rooms and spend the night.

If You Go: **Ten Thousand Waves** is about 4 miles northeast of Santa Fe on Hyde Park (Artist) Road, open daily from 10:00 A.M. to 9:30 P.M., later on weekends. Reservations preferred: **982-9304.** Another 13 miles up Hyde Park Road is the **Santa Fe Ski Area (982-4429).**

Insider Tip Avoid the crowds by skipping the busy weekend nights. If you're in Santa Fe often, a multiuse discount card is available. Also, you can use the mostly nude "community tub" and sauna for a much lower rate than the private facilities. During specified hours the community tub is reserved for women only.

7 *Best* Outdoor Market

For a truly "local" Santa Fe experience, come to its twice-weekly **Farmers' Market.** Only bonafide northern New Mexico growers are allowed to participate in the event, so you know your money is going to the person who planted, grew, and harvested the food you're buying. Besides the very freshest fruits and produce available—much of it certified organic—you can sample homemade breads, salsas, cheeses, chiles, jams, relishes, and more. Cut flowers and potted plants are also sold. Almost every weekend the market sponsors special events, ranging from a master gardener question-and-answer session to cooking demonstrations involving area farmers and restaurant chefs. There are strolling singers and musicians, too.

"The Farmer's Market folks are always friendly—and it's a terrific place to learn about cooking or gardening," says Nancy Porter, president of the Salvation Army board of directors, who, as a member of The Food Brigade, collects donated produce and delivers it to the poor and homeless.

If You Go: The **Santa Fe Area Farmers' Market (983-4098)** convenes Tuesday and Saturday from 7:00 to 11:30 A.M., in the Sanbusco Market Center parking lot, **500 Montezuma Street.** Nearby bakeries and restaurants are open for coffee and pastries.

8 *Best* Dancing

Swaying to a slow, Latin love song while Father Frank Pretto croons romantic endearments in your ear is a lesson in New Mexico incongruity. Why is the parish priest from Agua Fría's historic San Ysidro Church murmuring sweet nothings into a bandstand microphone?

"Why not?" counters Pretto. "Music is a wonderful gift from God and I love to celebrate it. Playing and singing is my joy, as is my Catholic faith."

Padre Pretto and members of his Latin dance band, Parranda, have entertained thousands of Santa Feans over the years, holding forth for four hours every Friday night in various hotels and nightclubs. A native of Panama who sings mostly in Spanish, Pretto's elaborate keyboard, synthesizer, and drum machine churn out the hottest merengue, cumbia, salsa, cha-cha, samba and bolero tunes this side of the border. Accompanying the good father is a trio of bongo, conga, and timbale players.

"Ours are rhythms from the heart," says Pretto, a slim, middle-aged man who sometimes takes a few turns on the dance floor between sets. "The melodies vibrate to the pulse of life."

Another twist in the tale is that Frank Pretto is from a Jewish family, of Spanish Sephardic descent. He attended a Catholic school, however, and sends part of his musical earnings to a church-sponsored soup kitchen back home in Colón, Panama's poorest city.

Pretto's addictive tunes and positive vibes not only attract salsa-loving Hispanics—of all faiths—but a substantial number of Anglos, Native Americans, Asians, and African-Americans as well.

"You don't need to be Latin to salsa," insists Kate Droney, a Santa Fe speech and language therapist of Irish descent. "You simply need to get loose and let the music take over. It's all in the hips!"

With a priest at the helm, this is a low-pressure party where everyone is welcome: young and old; single, couple, or groups. Birthday and wedding guests sometimes descend en masse, which makes for an even more festive occasion.

If You Go: Father Pretto plays from 9:00 P.M. to 1:00 A.M. every Friday (except during his three-week summer vacation and on Catholic holy days) at **Club Alegría (471-2324)**, on **Agua Fría**, 2 blocks north of Siler Road. Admission is $5 and liquor is served. It's best to come either early or late; the crowd peaks between 10:00 and 11:00 P.M.

Insider Tip
If you don't know Latin dance steps, come at 8:00 P.M. and take advantage of the free lessons. Beginners are always welcome.

9 Best Romantic Getaway

The **Don Gaspar Compound** is "secluded, beautifully appointed, and has six romantic rooms, some with whirlpool baths and fireplaces," enthuses Peggy van Hulsteyn, a Santa Fe author and travel journalist. "Magnificent gardens add to the ambiance."

The Compound is on a one-way side street within walking distance of the plaza. Van Hulsteyn, who has lived in Santa Fe long enough to remember when the chic Coyote Café was a Greyhound Bus station, adds that "the best non-touristy activities when you're staying at The Compound are to take a walk along the Santa Fe River [paralleling Alameda Street] and to hike in the nearby mountains."

If You Go: The **Don Gaspar Compound (986-8664)** is at **623 Don Gaspar.** Rates in 1996 were $85 to $220, double occupancy. Reservations are preferred.

10 Best Moderately Priced Accommodations

With the average price of a night's lodging well into three figures, Santa Fe can be an expensive city to visit. As a rule, the closer you are to the plaza, the more things cost—including hotel rooms. For those with a car (or who don't mind using Santa Fe's efficient bus or taxi services), a move to the outskirts can free up money for other diversions, such as eating and shopping.

Molly Seymour, who worked in hotel marketing here for years and is now a professional "B&B sitter," sends her out-of-town friends to any of the following comfortable, well-run, and moderately priced establishments:

- ◆ El Rey Inn (1862 Cerrillos Road, 982-1931)

- ◆ The Santa Fe Motel (510 Cerrillos Road, 982-1039)

- ◆ The Desert Inn (311 Old Santa Fe Trail, 982-1851)

- ◆ For the under-30 crowd, **Santa Fe Youth Hostel (1412 Cerrillos Road, 988-1153)**

- ◆ For families and groups, **Las Brisas (624 Galisteo, 982-5795)**

11 *Best* Place to See a Georgia O'Keeffe Painting

Gerald Peters, a prominent businessman and veteran trader in the Santa Fe art market for many years, says the best place to see an original painting by the legendary Georgia O'Keeffe is in his own **Gerald Peters Gallery.** Peters was O'Keeffe's dealer during the last decade of her life and has sold more of her paintings (175) than anyone else.

"O'Keeffe had a discriminating intellect and a clear conception of what she saw," says Peters. "She could reduce things to their absolute essence. Her images have no clutter and are very subtle."

The Peters Gallery is in the historic Mary Austin House, where author Mary Austin and photographer Ansel Adams collaborated on various projects. Willa Cather wrote her famous New Mexico novel, *Death Comes for the Archbishop,* in the library. The dealer expects to open a new contemporary gallery on Paseo de Peralta in 1997.

Peters advises that O'Keeffe's work can also be seen at **Owings Dewey Fine Art** and the **Museum of Fine Arts,** which houses a 13-piece collection. A **private O'Keeffe Museum** is scheduled to open at **217 Johnson Street**, in Santa Fe, during May 1997.

If You Go: Gerald Peters Gallery is at **439 Camino del Monte Sol, 988-8961. Owings Dewey Fine Art** is at **74 East San Francisco**, on the plaza, **982-6244.** The **Museum of Fine Arts** is at **107 East Palace, 827-4455.**

Insider Tip

The **Georgia O'Keeffe home** northwest of Santa Fe is now open for tours year-round, weather permitting. Visitors tour the interior and grounds of the rambling adobe house and studio where O'Keeffe lived from 1949 to 1984. (She died in Santa Fe in 1986.) You'll recognize the vistas that appear in some of O'Keeffe's most famous paintings and see furnishings much as she left them—even her homegrown herbs still sit on a kitchen shelf. Because O'Keeffe left stern orders that her home not be turned into a shrine or visitors' center, access is strictly controlled.

One-hour guided visits are by reservation **(685-4539)** every Tuesday, Thursday, and Friday. Interior/exterior tours cost $20 per person and are often booked months in advance. Tours of the grounds only are $15 (with a 20-person maximum). O'Keeffe's home is 48 miles from Santa Fe via US 84 in Abiquíu. Cameras are not allowed on tours and other restrictions apply.

12 *Best* Jogging Course

Elaine Pinkerton, author of *Santa Fe On Foot* and *The Santa Fe Trail By Bicycle,* says there's no better place to jog in town than *St. Catherine's Indian School,* especially in the peach-colored glow of sunset. The cross-country course has a rural feel, even though it's an easy walk from the plaza. Founded by wealthy Philadelphian Catherine Drexel in 1887, the school "speaks volumes about turn-of-the-century Santa Fe," says Pinkerton. "Before or after your run, check out the fascinating mural that dominates the Ed O'Brien Room: it depicts major events in the history of the Western Hemisphere."

If You Go: St. Catherine's Indian School **(982-1889)** is at **801 Griffin Street** and welcomes joggers.

Insider Tip Pinkerton's favorite bicycle rides are on the county roads south of town between the Santa Fe Downs Racetrack and the San Marcos Cafe on Hwy 14. A more ambitious trip is the 60-odd miles to Las Vegas via the Old Las Vegas Hwy and I-25 frontage roads.

13 *Best* Breakfast

Cafe Pasqual's, according to numerous surveys, serves some of the best food in a city that is crowded with fine restaurants. Breakfasts here are imaginative, delicious, and hearty, combining New Mexican traditions with Latin American departures and nineties' sensibilities.

"No cook I know has a keener palate or more creative approach to food," says Jean Anderson, author of *The New Doubleday Cookbook,* speaking of owner/chef Katharine Kagel. "Pasqual's not only remains my favorite Santa Fe restaurant, but also makes my U.S.A. top ten year after year."

Especially recommended are the Eggs Genovese and the tamales wrapped in banana leaves. There are almost always long lines, so be prepared to put your name on a list and take a long walk ... or eat at the "community table" and make new friends. Better yet, buy a copy of the excellent *Café Pasqual's Cookbook* written by Kagel, on sale at the cashier.

Other local breakfast favorites include **Tecolote Café, Guadalupe Café,** and **Harry's Roadhouse.** There are many excellent Sunday brunch choices as well, especially at local hotels.

If You Go: Café Pasqual's (983-9340) is at **121 Don Gaspar,** Tecolote at **1203 Cerrillos,** Guadalupe Café (982-9762) at **422 Old Santa Fe Trail,** and Harry's Roadhouse (989-4629) on the **Old Las Vegas Hwy,** one mile east of Old Pecos Trail.

Insider Tip For morning coffee, tea, and baked goods, local favorites include **Downtown Subscription** at 376 Garcia and **Pasale Bakery** at 328 South Guadalupe.

14 *Best* Lunch

Dave's Not Here derives its name, legend has it, from the original owner's unfortunate propensity for—*ahem*—tangling with the criminal justice system. Rather than explain their boss's sometimes prolonged absences, employees answered customer inquiries concerning his whereabouts with the unadorned and noncommittal, "Dave's not here." The name stuck, even though Dave eventually sold the place and is out of the picture.

Tucked in a tiny building in the heart of a working-class neighborhood (this is what most of Santa Fe used to look like), Dave's is locally famous for its humongous hamburgers, which approximate the dimensions of an unabridged dictionary and are invariably singled out in any local "best of" polls. A few years ago, Dave's agreed to serve a half-size burger, accurately perceiving that 90 percent of customers never finished their meal, garnished as it is with giant homemade French fries and gooey coleslaw. Other menu options include a recommended litany of New Mexican dishes, including wonderful chile rellenos and spicy blue-corn enchiladas. Prices are low and the ambiance funky. Be prepared to share a table and/or wait in the crowded entryway for a seat.

 Please don't ask current employees about the origin of the restaurant's name; they're very tired of explaining it.

Runners-up: **Molly's Kitchen & Lounge** is considered by many locals to be the best joint in town for classic New Mexican chile, pork tamales, and the place to go for that marinated pork adovada you've been dying to try. The interior is dark and simple, providing a welcoming, informal escape on those hot summer days when the sun seems merciless. There's also a full bar on the premises.

Carlos's Gosp'l Café, downtown in the First Interstate Plaza, is the best place to buy gospel music and eat a turkey sandwich. "They also serve the best pie in Santa Fe," proclaims Ann Yalman, an attorney and self-described lunch connoisseur. Yalman also recommends **Portare Via**'s chicken salad and **Il Vicino**'s vegetarian lasagna. **Celebrations** has the best chile relleno in town, according to long-time relleno critic Annie Muriel, who learned the fine points of New Mexican cuisine while attending high school in the tiny village of Hondo. (Other experts prefer **Tomasita's**, on Guadalupe.) The best green chile cheeseburger in town, according to a 1995 *Pasatiempo* poll, is served at **Bert's Burger Bowl.**

For upscale dining, there are many fine choices in the downtown area. Ask the locals what they consider "the best" at the time of your visit.

If You Go: Dave's Not Here (983-7060) is at **1115 Hickox, Molly's (983-7577)** at **1611 Calle Lorca, Carlos's Gosp'l Café (983 1841)** at **125 Lincoln, Portare Via (988-3886) at 500 Montezuma, Il Vicino (986-8700)** at **321 West San Francisco,** and **Celebrations (989-8904)** at **613 Canyon Road. Bert's Burger Bowl (982-0215)** is at **235 North Guadalupe.**

15 *Best* Dinner

Pranzo Italian Grill is that rarity in Santa Fe, a favorite among locals and visitors alike. And why not: the northern Italian food is superb, prices are reasonable, and seating options varied. During summer, you can dine *alfresco* on the front patio or upstairs balcony. (Pranzo is one of the few Santa Fe restaurants with a glimpse of the sunset.) In cooler months, there's an intimate dining room upstairs, equally cozy tête-á-tête nooks in the elegant bar, and your choice of booths or center-stage tables in the main downstairs room. As one would expect, the menu leans toward pastas, pizzas, and innovative Italian sauces. Fish and fowl are prepared expertly, and the wine list is impeccable. If your pet peeve is noisy restaurants, as is mine, you'll want to specify a booth when making your reservation and try to avoid peak dining hours. Located in the historic Railroad Yards District, Pranzo has a small annex (**Portare Via**) serving light lunches, pastries, tea and coffee next door at Sanbusco, an appealing indoor shopping center.

Runners-up: If cheap and cheerful is what you're after, you can't go wrong with the fiery New Mexican cuisine at **Baja Tacos,** a locally owned drive-in heavily favored by locals in the know—including former KUNM-FM Music Director Rachel Maurer and fictitious Albuquerque lawyer/sleuth Neil Hamel. Non-carnivores can feast on vegetarian versions of traditional chile-spiced dishes—the stuffed sopapillas are particularly delicious. Check out the deeply discounted "happy hour" prices. Also recommended for breakfast and lunch.

For the less adventurous, **The Palace** and **The Pink Adobe** are reliable stand-bys for good but non-fiery New Mexican and continental fare served in a pleasant atmosphere. **Fabio's Grill** is a runner-up in the Italian category.

For an elegant splurge, try **Café Escalera, Bistro 315, Geronimo,** or **SantaCafé,** all near the center of town. Prices are high, but the quality of food and service is excellent.

If You Go: Pranzo (984-2645) is at **540 Montezuma,** Baja Tacos at **2621 Cerrillos Road,** The Palace (982-9891) at **142 West Palace,** and **The Pink Adobe** (983-7712) at **406 Old Santa Fe Trail.** Café Escalera (989-8188) is at **130 Lincoln Avenue,** Bistro 315 (986-9190) at **315 Old Santa Fe Trail,** Geronimo (982-1500) at **724 Canyon Road,** SantaCafé (984-1788) at **231 Washington Avenue,** and Fabio's Grill (984-3080) at **327 West San Francisco Street.**

Vicinity of Santa Fe

16 Best Place to See Sculptures Being Made

Like her fellow sculptors from throughout the United States, California resident Gwyn Murrell visits **Shidoni** whenever she gets anywhere close to Santa Fe. A combination foundry, gallery, and outdoor sculpture garden, Shidoni is north of the city in the village of Tesuque.

"This is one of the greatest resources anywhere for sculptors and collectors of sculpture," says Murrell, whose own work is in museums and private collections all over the world. "Shidoni has evolved into a world-class casting facility. And what's fun about it is that visitors can learn firsthand about how these works of art are created."

Every Saturday, the public is invited to watch 2,000-degree molten bronze being poured into ceramic shell molds, one of several steps in the complex "lost wax" casting process. During other days of the week, you are welcome to tour the foundry during 15-minute work breaks that occur every couple of hours. Call ahead for exact times. There's usually something life-size or larger being worked on.

Murrell recalls that Shidoni (Navajo for "friendly greeting") was founded in 1971 as a two-man foundry catering only to local artists. It now employs 40 people and serves artists of international distinction.

Nestled at the foot of an old apple orchard, the foundry shows much of its work in two adjacent galleries (one traditional, the other contemporary) and on several acres of orchard grounds devoted to monumental sculpture. Visitors are invited to bring a picnic and enjoy the tranquil setting.

If You Go: Shidoni (988-8001) is 5 miles north of Santa Fe on **Bishop's Lodge Road.** From downtown, take Washington Street (the name soon changes to Bishop's Lodge Road) north and watch for a large sign on the left side of the road.

Insider Tip Come April, the apple trees are in radiant bloom and the temperatures are mild. If you're a bicyclist, the ride here is one of New Mexico's loveliest.

17 *Best* Flea Market

"Sooner or later, everybody in Santa Fe shows up at 'The Flea.'" This declaration by the late abstract Santa Fe painter, African art dealer, and bon vivant Don Fabricant stands the test of time. Sprawled across several acres of land owned by the Tesuque Pueblo, about 6 miles northwest of Santa Fe on US 84/285, **Trader Jack's Flea Market** is an eclectic institution where one can buy anything from used, plastic ice-cube trays to antique Tibetan religious artifacts, with plenty of chile ristras, fresh piñon nuts and silver-turquoise jewelry thrown in for good measure. There's a surprisingly good selection of antiquarian books, Latin American textiles, folk art, Persian carpets, precious gems, and even house plants.

"The Flea" is the closest thing to a Moroccan bazaar you are likely to find in North America. And, as in Morocco, the buyer is expected to haggle, bargain, and beware.

"Trader Jack's Flea Market is not about making money," opined Fabricant, who supplemented his irregular artist's income by trading goods at The Flea. "It's about socializing and observing humanity in its infinite variety."

If You Go: **Trader Jack's** is open from 8:00 A.M. to 5:00 P.M. every Friday, Saturday, and Sunday from (roughly) mid-March through November. No admission for customers.

18 *Best* Affordable Art

Hondo Hills silk-screen artist and retired Disney Studios animator Ken Peterson sends friends and relatives to **The White Hyacinth Gallery** for inexpensive "original art that is not junk!" The

White Hyacinth specializes in postcard- and poster-size reproductions of Southwest and Western-style art, as well as fine quality originals. Peterson, best known locally as the cartoonist who created Carlos Coyote (the mascot of Santa Fe's city-sponsored recycling program), encourages all visitors to "leave the city with at least one piece of original art. Santa Fe is one of the best places in the United States to buy something handmade and beautiful."

Runner-up: **Keshí,** a tiny gallery in the Santa Fe Village shopping arcade, sells hand-carved Native American fetish stones. Now privately owned, the store started a Zuni Indian cooperative and still attracts some of the pueblo's best fetish carvers, as well as Cochiti Pueblo's renowned Salvador Romero.

If You Go: The White Hyacinth Gallery (983-2832) is at **137 West San Francisco Street.** Keshí (989-8728) is at **227 Don Gaspar.**

Insider Tip Poster-size art reproductions are a good buy (around $50) in several Santa Fe galleries, notably **21st Century-Fox (215 West Water Street)** and **Contemporary Southwest Galleries (123 West Palace Avenue** and **201 Canyon Road).** While we're on this subject, a 1996 survey of *Santa Fe Reporter* readers rated **Copeland Rutherford Gallery (403 Canyon Road)** the site of Santa Fe's best art openings (they still serve food), and Nedra Matteucci's **Fenn Galleries (1075 Paseo de Peralta)** the best gallery overall. The best way to experience Santa Fe art, locals agree, is on a balmy Friday evening "art walk," when as many as 20 galleries may be celebrating the opening of new shows.

19 *Best* Scenic Route to Taos

If time is no object, take "The High Road." You can make it from Santa Fe to Taos in 75 minutes via "The Low Road," busy US 84 along the winding Río Grande, but El Camino Alto is much more scenic. It can take two hours or two days, depending on your mood.

At Chimayó, where the descendants of Spanish weavers ply their craft, be sure to visit **El Santuário de Chimayó,** a small

Catholic church nicknamed "the Lourdes of the Southwest" because of the belief that holy dirt scooped from the floor of the chapel has miraculous healing power. On Good Friday, thousands make a pilgrimage here to touch the sacred earth. In addition to three weaving studios and several fruit stands, there are several restaurants and B&Bs here. Try **Leona's,** next to the santuario, for good home-style New Mexican food (including multi-flavored tortillas), and **La Posada de Chimayó,** a four-room farmhouse B&B, for a night's rest in charming rural New Mexican style.

Also located in Chimayó, **Centinela Traditional Arts** is a gallery operated by Irvin and Lisa Trujillo in what was once the weaving studio of Irvin's father. This extraordinary enterprise is filled with wonderful samples of excellent local weavings and wood carvings. The better-known **Ortega's Weaving Shop** carries on an eight-generation family weaving tradition, selling handmade blankets, rugs, and clothing.

As you continue north on NM 76, you'll pass through the picturesque villages of Cordova (famous for its wood-carvers), Truchas, Ojo Sarco, Las Trampas, El Valle, and Peñasco, tiny Hispano farming communities snuggled into the verdant embrace of the Sangre de Cristo Mountains. Truchas, the most prosperous of these, now boasts two restaurants, three B&Bs, 10 galleries and gift shops, plus several residences where hand-crafted quilts, carvings, and weavings are sold.

"The Spanish settled the mountain villages of the High Road in the eighteenth century as part of a defense perimeter for the relative lowland communities," Dixon author and garlic grower Stanley Crawford explained in a 1993 New York Times essay. "[The High Road settlers] had to contend with normally harsh winters, Comanche bands, and colonial indifference."

These are hardy people who know how to survive. This is evident in their solidly built churches, efficient irrigation systems, and neatly cut woodpiles, as well as their tan, lined faces. If you travel this way, try to stop at a gallery, general store, or café and meet some of the High Roaders.

"I head for the nearest family restaurant and sit down to a bowl of hot green chile," Crawford wrote, "which helps reconcile me to being back on the Low Road again."

If You Go: Take the NM 503 exit north of Pojoaque off US 84 (about 15 miles north of Santa Fe) to begin the High Road through Nambé, following NM 520 to Chimayó. Take NM 76 from downtown Española for a shorter route through Santa Cruz. (The two roads intersect in Chimayó.) From Taos, follow US 64 about 15 miles east to Peñasco, then turn south on NM 76. **La Posada de Chimayó (351-4605)** is on NM 76, with 1996 rates from $80 to $125, double occupancy. **Ortega's (351-4215)** is open daily at the intersection of NM 520 and NM 76 in Chimayó. **Centinela Traditional Arts (351-2180)** is north of the village on NM 76.

20 *Best* Alternatives to Bandelier National Monument

Ancient Anasazi rock art.

See the **Puyé Cliffs** and avoid the crowds that usually overwhelm nearby Bandelier National Monument. You will climb wooden ladders among very similar ancient Indian constructions—caves and other cliff dwellings inhabited until 1577 by the ancestors of today's Pueblo tribes, in this instance the Santa Clara. There's a 740-room abandoned village and a reconstructed ceremonial kiva at the top of Puyé Mesa, which has a fine view of the Española Valley.

Also worth visiting is the **Tsunkawi unit of Bandelier National Monument**, a small and separate enclave of the main park.

Tsunkawi protects the ruins of an old mesa-top village and many cave dwellings that are carved into the soft volcanic tufa rock of nearby cliffs. It's fascinating to walk along pathways that have been worn 18 inches deep into the tufa by the erosion of human feet.

"Although it was the height of mid-August tourist season," noted *Cheap Thrills* author and *Albuquerque Journal* reporter Frank Zoretich in an article about Tsunkawi, "I encountered only three other visitors during the more than two hours I spent there."

An adventurous tourist gets a close-up look at the Anasazi Ruins at Bandelier National Monument.

If You Go: The **Puyé Cliffs (753-7330)** are open from 9:00 A.M. to 6:00 P.M. daily for a $5 fee (seniors and children, $4). There's no charge for still pictures but a camcorder permit costs $10. A dirt road goes to the top of Puyé Mesa for those who don't wish to climb ladders from below. Take NM 30 from Española or Santa Fe, then head west about 11 miles on Santa Clara Canyon Road.

Because of budget cuts, **Tsunkawi (627-3861)** has irregular hours and is sometimes closed. There are restrooms and picnic facilities here but no other services. Entrance fee: $3. From Santa Fe, take US 285 north to Pojoaque, then NM 502 west toward Los Alamos, and NM 4 south about 0.25 mile to the Tsunkawi trailhead. The main entrance to Bandelier is about 12 miles south on NM 4.

21 *Best* View of the Río Grande

White Rock Overlook—also called Overlook Park—is a spectacular aerie on a basalt cliff high above the roiling, frothy Río Grande. There are a few picnic tables and a hiking trail that winds to the river below. This is a terrific place to watch the vast New Mexico sky against a backdrop of tall mountains and deep canyons.

"Go while you still can," advises geographer and author Don Usner. "The New Mexico Highway Department is considering construction of a new road through the gorge that would remove this overlook."

If You Go: Take NM 502 west toward Los Alamos, then follow NM 4 for 4 miles to the small community of White Rock and look for the **Overlook Park** directional sign. You'll drive through a residential neighborhood to get there.

Insider Tip

If you want to see another side of the local landscape, visit the **Bradbury Science Museum (667-4444)** in the town of Los Alamos (at **15th and Central**). You'll see exhibits outlining the history of the atomic bomb, born here in 1945. So secret was research surrounding this device that Los Alamos was closed to unauthorized visitors until 1957. Open daily, admission free.

Los Alamos also has one of New Mexico's few outdoor **ice-skating rinks,** open daily during the coldest winter months for a $3.50 adult admission ($2 for children). The rink is in a canyon off West Road, near downtown. Skates can be rented for a small fee.

22 *Best* Place to Experience El Camino Real

Las Golondrinas is a historic *paraje*, or stopping point, along El Camino Real, "the royal road" between Santa Fe and Mexico City that served as New Mexico's critical link with Spanish authorities for more than two centuries. Because of an abundant supply of spring water and grass, travelers would spend the night here on their way to or from Santa Fe, a day's journey to the north.

Las Golondrinas was a private ranch throughout much of this century, but the land eventually became available to those interested in preserving New Mexican history. Indeed, this "living museum" is one of the few places where one has a real sense of what everyday life was like here before 1900.

On permanent display is a collection of historical artifacts and several old buildings moved here from other parts of the state, including a shepherd's hut, *morada* (meeting place of the *Penitientes* religious order), and two water-driven flour mills, one from Spanish colonial days and a larger one from the United States territorial era.

"The big horizontal mill wheel was repaired a few years back and still grinds wheat, as does the horizontal millstone," explains Louann Jordan, curator of programs for the museum. "We interpret a period of time from 1700 through the 1800s and try to keep our costumes and buildings as authentic as they can be."

An old Spanish hacienda has been converted into a museum shop and exhibit area, with new displays every other year. Recent exhibitions have dealt with the history of El Camino Real (dating from 1598) and the Old Santa Fe Trail (started in 1821) as well as the changes in New World agriculture wrought by Spanish colonists.

Scheduled events include Spring, Summer, and Harvest festivals, during the first weekends of June, August, and October, respectively, plus a wine festival (July) and Civil War reenactment (May). Dance, music, craft displays, and food booths accompany these events ... and sometimes costumed villagers will demonstrate what life was like here two centuries ago.

If You Go: You can visit **Las Golondrinas** on your own, from 10:00 A.M. to 4:00 P.M. Wednesday through Sunday, June through September. Guided tours by appointment **(473-4169)** from April 1 through October 31. **El Rancho de las Golondrinas (471-2261)** is 15 miles south of Santa Fe in the village of La Cienega at **334 Los Pinos Road.** Take Exit 276 off I-25 and follow the signs. Admission fees are $1.50 for children, $2.50 for teens and seniors, and $3.50 for adults. Festival admissions slightly higher.

Chapter 3
Taos and Vicinity

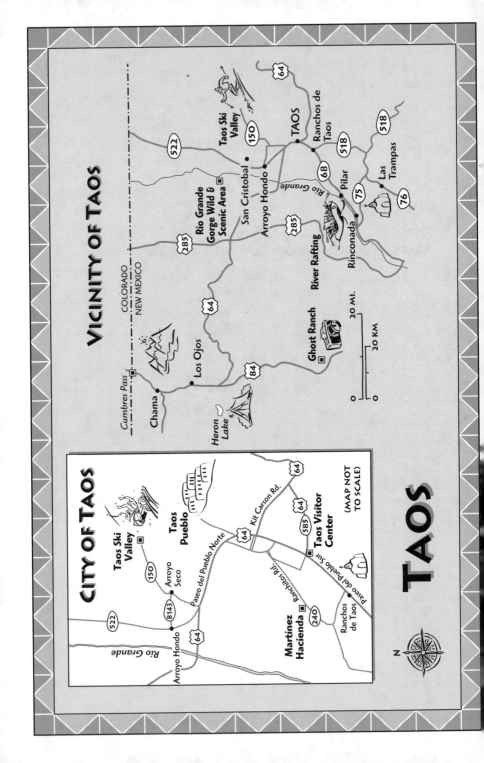

What's Best about Taos

The name Taos carries certain connotations: artists, adobes, an ancient Indian pueblo, downhill skiing, whitewater rafting. For consumers of popular culture, the word may conjure up the old *McCloud* TV series, in which actor Dennis Weaver played a fish-out-of-water sheriff transplanted to the big city; or *The Milagro Beanfield War*, written by Taoseño John Nichols and made into a movie by occasional New Mexico resident Robert Redford.

Like most stereotypes, each image harbors a grain of truth. For example, Taos is indeed an art colony—home to more than 1,000 artists and 100 galleries—and it is a ski bum's paradise—with average annual accumulations of more than 320 inches on the slopes of nearby Taos Ski Valley. But at least two other defining characteristics also make Taos special: its great physical beauty and its relative isolation. Spread across a broad, arid plain between the snowcapped Sangre de Cristo Mountains and the deep canyon of the Río Grande, Taos is inhabited by people who take pride in their rugged individualism and confident self-reliance. More than 130 miles from the nearest major airport and accessible mainly by winding two-lane roads, living in Taos for many residents reflects a deliberate choice.

Despite its long human history—Pueblo Indians have lived here for more than 1,000 years—the town of Taos is home to only about 8,000 year-round residents, with a comparable number scattered around the city's wide perimeter. This is a truly multicultural community, composed of Native Americans (members of the Taos tribe), Hispanos (whose Spanish ancestors began arriving about four centuries ago), and European-descended Americans (called Anglos throughout New Mexico). What binds them together is a love and respect for Taos traditions in fine art, architecture, and culture. There seems to be not only an acceptance but an encouragement of diversity in lifestyle, language, and viewpoint. One also senses a common appreciation of the area's spectacular natural beauty, which serves as a constant backdrop.

"There's always an extensive landscape to be discovered in a flower, an apple or a trout; in a culvert, or in the shadows of a church wall," novelist John Nichols has written about his adopted hometown. The Taos skies, he observed, are "unbearably bloated with an infinite profusion of clouds, weather, and wanton mood changes."

Even though it is rich in beauty and tradition, the Taos economy is based largely on tourism, art, and subsistence agriculture, which seldom yield affluence for those involved. This may explain the love/hate relationship toward tourists exhibited by some Taoseños, who are cordial and welcoming to visitors, but prefer they not stay too long or, worse yet, move in. I've been offered this as a partial explanation for Taos's notoriously congested summer streets and indifferent service: locals are afraid that if they make tourists too comfortable, they'll never leave.

Like Santa Fe, the plaza and downtown core of Taos have been turned over mostly to businesses that cater to visitors. And as in Santa Fe, the most touted destinations, such as **Taos Pueblo** and **Millicent Rogers Museum,** are worth a visit. Some other attractions, however, including D. H. Lawrence's "erotic" paintings at the La Fonda Hotel and Kit Carson's grave, aren't worth bothering with. What's best about Taos are the smaller and more unusual shops, galleries, and public buildings downtown, and the nooks and crannies of the surrounding streets. "If time permits," recommends El Prado art appraiser Jim Parsons, "visit an artist's studio." Parsons also suggests picking up a copy of the *Taos News,* published every Thursday, and checking out the *Tempo* section.

My own advice is to come to Taos during the off-season, preferably early October or late May, when the crowds are small and the weather more conducive to leisurely walks. As always, you should get off the beaten path. Better yet, get lost!

For the purposes of this book, the Taos area includes all of Taos County, plus the northern portions of adjacent Río Arriba County. Communities within this region include Taos, Ranchos de Taos, Arroyo Hondo, Arroyo Seco, Questa, Tres Piedras, Chama, and Tierra Amarilla.

Taos is about 70 miles (75 minutes) north of Santa Fe via US 68. If you're taking the longer and more scenic "high road," NM 76, allow at least half an hour more. Once you're in Taos there's a public transportation system serving major destinations, including the ski area. Transportation options from the Albuquerque airport include the **Pride of Taos** and **Faust shuttles** as well as the **TNM&O bus.** Entering Taos from the south, you'll see a **visitors' center (800-732-TAOS)** on the right side of US 68 where it intersects with US 64. The staff here are friendly and well informed.

1 Best Private Homes Open to the Public

A stroll through the **Fechin, Harwood, and Blumenschein Houses** takes the visitor back to this community's early years as a twentieth-century art colony, when Anglo painters—mostly East Coast urbanites—first reveled in the natural beauty and quiet solitude of Taos Valley.

In 1898, New York painter Ernest Blumenschein broke an axle near Questa on the horse-drawn wagon he and a friend were using to traverse northern New Mexico. Blumenschein sought help in the nearest town, which turned out to be Taos. Instantly enchanted by the place, the artist soon persuaded his wife, the acclaimed painter Mary Shepherd, to visit him. Mary, too, fell is love with Taos and in 1919 the couple moved into an adobe home built in 1797. "Blumy" became one of the original members of the Taos Society of Artists, the influential group that founded the first so-called art colony here.

"These were all talented and diverse artists who came together with the distinct purpose of promoting each other's work and advancing the standards of American art," says David Witt, one of the New Mexico's foremost art historians. "They would travel all over the United States with exhibitions of their paintings, providing many people with their first inkling of what New Mexico looked like."

The Blumenschein House is now a museum and gallery specializing in twentieth-century Taos artists. It is full of many of the family's furnishings, including handcrafted New Mexican furniture,

European antiques, and Asian prints. You enter the house through the kitchen, where a dining table beckons and old cereal boxes still sit in the cupboard. The painting studio in the middle of the house boasts the first oak floor in Taos, which made it popular as an informal dance hall.

Further down Ledoux Street is the **Harwood Foundation Museum,** where the creations of realist and modernist Taos artists are featured in the late collector Burt Harwood's old home. Memorable items in the collection include wood carvings by Patrociño Barela, paintings by Victor Higgens and other members of the Taos Society of Artists, as well work by such contemporary painters as Agnes Martin.

"There are more than 1,200 art items in our permanent collection and 17,000 photographs," explains Witt, curator of the Harwood and author of *The Life and Art of Patrociño Barela*. "Besides the permanent displays, we mount about six new exhibitions each year."

The University of New Mexico operates the Harwood in order to research and display the art history of the Taos area, focusing primarily on the twentieth century. A few blocks away is the home of another important early member of the Taos art community: Nicolai Fechin.

Nine years after the 1917 Russian Revolution, renowned sculptor, painter and wood-carver Nicolai Fechin emigrated from his homeland to live in Taos. Over the next six years he created a marvelous marriage of Russian imperial and Spanish colonial artistic sensibilities that delights the senses. The adobe house, remodeled by Fechin in 1928, is a work of art in itself. All the richly detailed interior woodwork was carved by Fechin— the son of a carver of wooden icons—as a respite from painting, which he considered his primary occupation. A hallmark of Fechin's architectural design is the clever combination of form and function: dressing screens look like dragons, door-knockers are shaped like bears.

The graceful house now serves as a gallery, with changing exhibitions competing for attention with a permanent display of Fechin's Asian art. During late September each year many of the artist's paintings are hung temporarily. Fechin, who moved from Taos to New York after a 1933 divorce, eventually relocated to California, where he died in 1970. The house is owned by his daughter, Eya, who lives in separate quarters on the property. In 1996 an 85-room hotel, **The Fechin Inn (751-1000)**, was opened behind the main house as well as a restaurant in front. Both include architectural elements inspired by Fechin's work.

If You Go: **The Fechin House (758-1710)**, at **277 Paseo del Pueblo Norte,** is open from 1:00 to 5:00 P.M., Wednesday through Sunday, and admission is $3. **The Blumenschein House (758-0505)** is open daily year-round (except Thanksgiving, Christmas, and New Year's Day), from 9:00 A.M. to 5:00 P.M. Admission is $4 adults, $2.50 children. It is at **222 Ledoux Street,** two blocks southwest of the Taos Plaza. **The Harwood House (758-9826)** is at **238 Ledoux Street** ($2 admission weekdays from 10:00 A.M. to 5:00 P.M. and Saturdays 10:00 A.M. to 4:00 P.M.; Tuesdays free, closed major holidays).

2 *Best* Famous Pueblo

Although technically not *in* the town of Taos, the pueblo of Taos might as well be. It is only two miles north of the plaza and has loomed like a shadow over its European-dominated neighbor since the latter's founding by Spanish settlers in 1617. If nothing else, one must give **Taos Pueblo** and its people applause for their endurance. Founded a thousand or more years ago, the two multistoried adobe apartment houses that dominate the community have looked much the same since Coronado and his conquistadors visited them in 1540. Small wonder, then, that the Spanish later adapted the Indians' (and Moors') mud-and-straw construction techniques to build their own houses, many of which have now lasted for two centuries or more.

"A visit to Taos Pueblo is the best way to get a powerful and immediate sense of Native American history and culture in this area," says R. C. Gorman, a celebrated Navajo painter who lives in nearby El Prado. "The architecture is amazing, the artwork wonderful, and the setting magnificent, but be sure to respect the privacy of those who call this their home."

As exciting and awe-inspiring as it is to see the venerable Taos Pueblo structures still in use after so many years, there is something disconcerting about coming here as a tourist. After all, how would you feel if cars and buses pulled up in your driveway all day, every day, disgorging hundreds of strangers who snapped pictures of where and how you lived? Would you like to be asked constantly by someone you'd never met if he or she could take *your* picture? One can rationalize that the pueblo invites tourism, but is it sufficient payment for a certain loss of dignity? No matter, there's no talk of closing the pueblo to tourists—who bring considerable income to the tribe—and it remains a must-see destination simply because of the complex experience of being there.

Beyond the buildings themselves, and the wonderful play of light and shadow against their textured surfaces, there's not much to see in Taos Pueblo, unless you come on a special occasion or would like to buy something from one of the many Indians selling jewelry, food, or drinks. Many of the pueblo's buildings and 95,000 acres are off-limits, and you shouldn't enter any homes without being invited. (If invited, it's an opportunity you shouldn't pass up.)

If You Go: **Taos Pueblo (758-8626),** about 2 miles north of the Taos Plaza, is open daily from 8:00 A.M. to 5:00 P.M. Visitors are subject to a $5-per-car admission fee and a $5 fee for still photography. Higher fees are assessed for videotaping and sketching. Tours are offered by members of the tribe, who can summarize the pueblo's long history.

Insider Tip The best time to visit Taos Pueblo is during a dance ceremonial or on a feast day. For example, on the two concurrent feast days of San Geronimo (September 29–30), young male members of the tribe try to shimmy up one of several tall poles, slicked with grease, to untie bundles of food and trinkets tied to the very top. This lighthearted spectacle, which includes foot races and the dancing and cavorting of painted clowns, lasts an entire afternoon. Meanwhile, vendors sell food, drinks, and artwork along the Río Taos, which flows through the center of the pueblo. Other special days are December 25, January 1, January 6, and July 10– 12. Photography during dances is not allowed.

3 *Best* Horseback Riding

Cantering along a shadowy trail that winds among the steep, forested folds of their tribe's majestic Taos Mountain, the pack of well-disciplined horses led by Storm Star Gómez is reined to a dusty halt in an undulating meadow carpeted with wildflowers and smelling of spring. The Taos Pueblo Indian pushes back his hat and gestures over his shoulder.

"This is where we turn around," declares Storm Star, who with his wife Sandi guides equestrian trips through this Native-owned wilderness. "Up ahead lies our tribe's sacred Blue Lake, a place where we make ritual pilgrimages—and where outsiders are not allowed."

The horses lower their necks and graze happily in the grama grass, while Sandi and Storm Star tell their visitors about the Taos Pueblo's long— but ultimately successful—legal battle to reclaim Blue Lake from the U.S. Forest Service. As the two-hour ride continues, the Gómezes will answer questions about the tribe's famous San Lorenzo Day Festival, its annual rabbit hunt, and the impressive adobe architecture that dominates one of the longest continually inhabited communities in the United States. By the time they return to the couple's modest ranch house, the non-Indian riders will have not only seen some of the prettiest backcountry in New Mexico—all off-limits to unescorted visitors—but have also learned firsthand what makes this 95,000-acre pueblo so special. It's a memorable experience that can't be duplicated at any of the state's two dozen other reservations.

If You Go: **Taos Indian Horse Ranch (800 659-3210)** is operated by Storm Star and Sandi Gómez, who are happy to provide equestrian instruction. Three types of excursions are available: an "easy" ride designed for moms and kids ($32 each for up to an hour); intermediate ($65, two hours, ages 8 and older); and advanced ($95, a "spirited" two-hour trip). Rides are by appointment, year-round, and 24-hour notice is preferred.

_4_ *Best* Museum

Millicent Rogers, a former Manhattan fashion model and designer, fell in love with Taos and moved to town in 1947. During the 1940s and 1950s, this energetic woman with a keen eye for beauty amassed one of the country's finest collections of Native American and Spanish colonial art, including paintings by Dorothy Brett and bowls made by the famous San Ildefonso Pueblo potters Julián and María Martínez. After her death in 1953, Rogers's 1,200-item art collection became the basis for what remains of New Mexico's flagship private museum, the **Millicent Rogers Museum,** located north of Taos in an old adobe home. The exhibits are well curated and provide a first-rate overview of the artistic accomplishments of the state's Native American, Hispano, and Anglo residents. There's also a high-quality gift shop on the premises.

"It's the best museum in Taos and one of the best in the state," maintains James Parsons, an art appraiser and dealer specializing in the work of northern New Mexico's tri-cultural arts tradition.

Runner-up: The spectacular **Van Vechten-Lineberry Taos Art Museum,** which claims to be the only museum in New Mexico where you can see the work of all of the original members of the Taos Society of Artists, who thrived here from 1916 through the mid-1930s. It also displays work by contemporary Taos painters as well as the late Duane Van Vechten, first wife of art patron Edwin Lineberry, who cofounded this state-of-the-art facility with his second wife, Novella.

If You Go: The nonprofit **Millicent Rogers Museum (758-2462)** is 4 miles north of Taos and open daily from 10:00 A.M. to 5:00 P.M. (except Mondays from November to March and major holidays). Admission is $4 for adults, $3 for seniors, and $3 for children under 17. Take NM 522 north of Taos toward the blinking light intersection (at US 64); follow the signs immediately before US 64 (at the Texaco station) to the museum. The **Van Vechten-Lineberry Museum (758-2690)** is immediately north of the Kachina Lodge at **501 North Pueblo Road.** Open Tuesday–Friday from 11:00 A.M. to 4:00 P.M., Saturday–Sunday from 1:30 to 4:00 P.M. Admission is $5 for adults, $3 for children and seniors.

Insider Tip

Buy a Museum Association of Taos pass and see all seven local museums for $18 (a savings of $8 over purchasing tickets individually).

5 *Best* Small-Scale Balloon Fiesta

An intimate, scaled-down alternative to the giant Albuquerque Balloon Fiesta is the annual **Taos Mountain Balloon Rally,** which takes place the fourth weekend of October in Taos. Visitors can view two mass ascensions on the Saturday and Sunday mornings of the event. There is also a gala **Balloon Ball,** parade, picnic, raffle party, and Sunday brunch plus tether rides for children of all ages. On Saturday evening you can witness a "balloominaria," when pilots light up their balloons to look like the holiday season luminarias and farolitos northern New Mexico is famous for.

"Best of all," says Don White, a balloonist who's flown in many parts of the state, "the viewing areas are not crowded and the ambiance is relaxed. Balloonists can take the time to answer questions and, if you're lucky, give free rides. The view of Taos Valley and its surroundings," White adds, "is superb."

If You Go: Most **Balloon Fiesta** events are free and take place at **Weimer Field;** for information, **758-8321.** If you'd like to go ballooning in Taos at other times of the year, call **Paradise Hot Air Balloons** at **758-2378,** which offers trips into the Río Grande Gorge as well as special full-moon flights. Prices start at about $130 per person.

6 *Best* Breakfast

For breakfast in Taos, try the centrally located **Bent Street Deli,** which offers hearty breakfasts in a pleasant atmosphere that includes a heated patio. The best early-morning burrito is at **The Burrito Wagon,** insists Philip Bareiss, owner of the Bareiss Galley. "It's a fantasy of potatoes, egg, green chile, and perhaps ham, chorizo, or bacon, snuggled into a flour tortilla." Bareiss is a connoisseur of "burrito wagons," of which there are at least ten in Taos. "They offer an authentic taste and good quality not found in restaurants," he says.

Susan's Grill is a good family restaurant with reasonable prices. For that early-morning hit of caffeine, stop at **Caffe Tazza,** which serves home-style breakfasts as well as delicious coffee drinks. If you're in the mood for "the best high-calorie splurge," as Navajo artist R. C. Gorman puts it, head north of town to the village of Arroyo Seco, where **Casa Fresen** makes sinfully rich pastries as well as delicious breads, gourmet lunches, and coffee drinks.

If You Go: **Bent Street Deli (758-5787)** is open for breakfast, lunch, and dinner at **120 Bent Street**, as is **Caffe Tazza (758-8706)**, at **122 East Kit Carson Road**. The Burrito **Wagon** (no phone) is behind the Centinel Bank on **South Santa Fe Road**. Susan's Grill **(758-2085)** is at **1128 Paseo del Pueblo Sur**. The **Casa Fresen Bakery (776-2969)** is at **482 NM 150 (Ski Valley Road)** in Arroyo Seco, open daily from 7:30 A.M. to 6:00 P.M.

7   Best Lunch

If you like authentic New Mexican food, check out **Mante's Chow Cart.** The name derives from this humble drive-in restaurant's even humbler origins as a pushcart on the Taos Plaza more than 20 years ago. Owner Mante Chacón developed a following among locals as he pushed his "chow cart" from one street corner to the next. Eventually, a big restaurant took over Chacón's favorite spot on the plaza and a permanent location was found nearby at an abandoned hamburger stand. Recommended are the tortilla-wrapped chile rellenos stuffed with beans and sour cream (a Mante Chacón creation). The chalupas are also very good and retired ballet dancer Jack Kauflin swears "the best ever" breakfast burritos are found here.

Slightly more expensive is **El Patio de Taos,** on the northwest corner of the plaza. It serves lunch and dinner, and occupies the oldest building in town, dating back to a 1600s trading post. The New Mexican dishes are your best bet. Also recommended is **El Taoseño,** on the main road south of the plaza, which serves the town's best posole and has a friendly lounge frequented by locals.

For excellent New York-style deli items, you can't beat **Murray's** on the southeast side of the plaza. Eat in or take out. **The Renegade Café** is a fine bar and grill 5 miles north of town on Ski Valley Road. It serves all three meals, combining Southwest flavors with an Italian influence.

If You Go: **Mante's (758-3632)** is at **402 Paseo del Pueblo Sur. El Patio (758-2121)** is on **Terasina Lane,** between the plaza and Bent Street. **El Taoseño (758-4142)** is at **819 Paseo del Pueblo Sur, Murray's (758-4205)** at **115 East Plaza,** and **The Renegade (776-1777)** at the **Quail Ridge Inn** on **Ski Valley Road.**

8 *Best* Dinner

Two popular Taos standbys that have plenty of Southwest-style ambiance are **The Apple Tree** and **Lambert's.** You pay for that ambiance of course, but the food's not bad either, with Lambert's having the edge on account of its innovative, oft-changing menu. The Apple Tree, located in a two-story building that used to be one of the town's many whorehouses, has a pleasant outdoor patio that is well suited to Sunday brunch. Lunch and dinner are also served. Lambert's, which also has outdoor seating, is open for dinner only. Some of the best food in Taos is served at **Villa Fontana,** although the quality of service generally doesn't match the steep prices. The atmosphere is elegant and quiet.

Philip Bareiss swears by the high-energy (read noisy) **Trading Post Café** in the historic Ranchos general store. Delicious Italian and creative nouvelle cuisine are available for lunch and dinner, Monday through Saturday. "The food is interesting and the service fantastic—they treat everyone like a movie star," says Bareiss. "The Trading Post is unpretentious and locals love it. Don't look for New Mexican food or chile, though—they don't serve it."

For a sunset view that goes on forever, try **The Stakeout,** a ranch-style bar and dinner-only grill on the road to Santa Fe. Specializing in steak and seafood, it won the 1993 "Taste of Taos" award for "best food." For New Mexico's best homegrown beer, have a cold one at **Eske's Brew Pub,** about a block off the plaza. Eske's also serves wholesome meals; open daily from noon to 10:30 p.m. Worthy of their reputation are the ever-popular **Doc Martin's** and **Sagebrush Inn.**

If You Go: The Apple Tree (758-1900) is at **123 Bent Street**. **The Trading Post Café (758-5089)** is 4 miles south of the plaza at the intersection of US 64 and NM 518 in Ranchos de Taos. **Lambert's (758-1009)**, at **309 Paseo del Pueblo Sur,** serves dinner only. **Villa Fontana (758-5800)** is on US 522 a few miles north of the plaza. **The Stakeout (758-2041)** is 9 miles south of Taos on NM 68. **Eske's Brew Pub (758-1517)** is at **106 Des Georges Lane**. **Doc Martin's (758-1977)** is in the **Taos Inn** on the plaza, and the **Sagebrush Inn (758-2254)** is at **1508 Paseo del Pueblo Sur.**

Insider Tip

If you run into John Nichols, the *Milagro Beanfield War* author who's lived here since 1969, don't pester him for a restaurant suggestion. "People are always asking me where to eat in Taos," says Nichols, "and I never have any idea 'cause I hardly ever go out."

9 *Best* B&Bs

Taos County bills itself as "the bed-and-breakfast capital of the Southwest" and the claim rings true. There were nearly 40 at last count, with something for every budget and aesthetic preference.

Molly Seymour—a professional "inn-sitter" whose business is taking care of B&Bs while managers take a breather, is especially fond of **Little Tree**—about 10 miles north of the Taos Plaza. "It's a place to slow down and enjoy the quiet of the country," says Seymour, "and the 360-degree views are really spectacular." Prices are modest and you'll get a full breakfast.

In an informal poll of local B&B operators, **Casa de las Chimenas** (House of the Chimneys) emerged as the best choice for those seeking romance and luxury. Everything—from the fine linens to the corner fireplaces—invites cozying up with someone you love. The old adobe is on a quiet side street within walking distance of the plaza.

For skiers and other outdoor sports enthusiasts, you can't do better than **Salsa del Salto,** an architectural gem near Arroyo Seco. Owners Mary Hockett and Dadou Mayer are award-winning skiers and Mary is an accomplished equestrian as well. A native of France and longtime Taos Ski Valley ski instructor, Dadou supervises Salsa del Salto's famous gourmet breakfast while Albuquerque-raised Mary is the inn's expert baker. There's a swimming pool, hot tub, and tennis court on the premises.

If You Go: Contact **Little Tree (776-8467)** at **Box 960, El Prado, NM 87529. Casa de las Chimenas (758-4777)** is at **405 Córdoba Lane. Salsa del Salto (800-530-3097)** is on **Ski Valley Road,** about 1 mile north of Arroyo Seco. If these are full, call the **Taos B&B Association (800-876-7857)** for information on accommodations among its members.

Vicinity of Taos

10 Best Downhill Skiing

"The simple facts about Taos remain unchanged," declared *Snow Country* magazine in a 1993 review of **Taos Ski Valley**. "The terrain is varied and often challenging, the sunny weather is a kick, and there probably isn't a better place in the country to learn to ski."

Although it's harder to get to than many other Rocky Mountain venues, Taos Ski Valley is consistently rated the best downhill ski resort in New Mexico, and one of the best in the entire United States. The slopes receive an average of 320 inches of white stuff each winter (plus artificial snow), and there is something for skiers of every ability.

"Taos has quite a few beginner, intermediate, and particularly expert runs, plus it's blessed with great snow," says Dan Gibson, who has skied in New Mexico since he was six and writes about the state's skiing for *Powder, Ski World,* and other publications. "The ultimate powder skiing in New Mexico is found off either Highline or West Basin Ridges at Taos.

"The best bar and best restaurant are at the **Hotel St. Bernard**," adds Gibson. "It's also my favorite place to stay."

If You Go: Lodging, restaurants, childcare, and rental equipment are provided in a comfortable complex at the base of 12,481-foot Kachina Peak. Taos Ski Valley is surrounded by the Carson National Forest, 15 miles northeast of the town of Taos via NM 150 (also called Ski Valley Road). Skiing information: **800-776-1111** or **776-2233. Hotel St. Bernard** information: **776-2251.**

11 *Best* Mysterious Painting

In Ranchos de Taos—once a community separate from Taos that has now begun to merge with the latter—generations of visitors have been captivated by a 19th-century religious painting by Henri Ault called *The Shadow of the Cross*, which hangs in the offices of the historic San Francisco de Asís Church. When the lights are turned off, the ghostly image of a cross appears above the shoulder of Jesus. When the lights go on, the cross disappears. The painting was made before radium or luminescent paints were in use and researchers have been unable to explain the glow in scientific terms. The devout, meanwhile, attribute its presence to spiritual sources. You decide.

San Francisco de Asís—commonly known as the **Ranchos de Taos Church**—was built in 1772 and became famous during the 1930s, after New Mexico painter Georgia O'Keeffe used it as the subject for several paintings. The structure's massive windowless adobe walls, wide buttresses, and tall bell towers make it a favorite subject for photographers, especially as the light and shadows shift along its mud-brown surfaces in early morning and late afternoon. Ansel Adams and Laura Gilpin are among those who have captured the church's massive shape and somber shading.

"The building is a work of art," says acclaimed photographer Paula Riff. "It's my favorite adobe structure in all of New Mexico."

Inside the church are many old paintings and *retablos* (painted wooden altar pieces), as well as a huge cedar carving of St. Francis of Assisi. Visitors are welcome, but remember that this is an active church where services are still conducted.

If You Go: **San Francisco de Asís Church (758-2754)** is open daily from 9:00 A.M. to 4:30 P.M. It's in St. Francis Plaza, 4 miles south of Taos on US 84 (NM 68). A slide show and lecture describing the place are presented several times a day in the church office, where there's also a gift shop. Admission is free except for large groups ($1 per person).

12 *Best* Hacienda

The 21-room **Martínez Hacienda,** which dates back to the 1780s, is a museum that provides a glimpse of what life among the upper classes might have been like when Spain and Mexico ruled New Mexico. It's one of the few restored Spanish colonial homes that's open to the public. Built in typical adobe compound style, the hacienda has no exterior windows but within its walls are two pleasant courtyards where family members could relax with some measure of security. The rambling complex was built by Don Antonio Severino Martínez, an early mayor of Taos and a prosperous merchant.

Built like a fortress in order to ward off the Apaches and Comanches, historian Felix Gutierrez says the Martínez adobe is "a classic example of what hacienda life was like in the late 1700s."

As part of an ongoing "living museum" program, the house sometimes features live demonstrations of traditional New Mexico weaving, furniture making, *santo* carving, and smithing. The surrounding rooms are furnished with antiques and reproductions appropriate to the region's Spanish and Mexican eras. Note the four horses grazing along the Río Pueblo: they are directly descended from Spanish Barb stock brought to the New World by the conquistadors more than four centuries ago.

If You Go: The **Martínez Hacienda (758-0505)** is open daily from 9:00 A.M. to 5:00 P.M. for a small admission charge. The house is about 2 miles west of Taos on Lower Ranchitos Road (NM 240) or 4 miles west of Ranchos de Taos on NM 240. Late in September there's a weekend "trade fair" here that recreates similar events held during the nineteenth century on the Taos Plaza.

13 *Best* Flashback to the Sixties

Actor and part-time Taos resident Dennis Hopper called it "an important part of the sixties's history." The late LSD guru Timothy Leary said, "I can't wait to come back."

The **New Buffalo** is not your usual country inn … rather, it is a funky, 1990s version of a classic 1960s institution: the commune. New Buffalo has come a long way since its pseudo-documentary depiction in Hopper's acclaimed 1969 film, *Easy Rider*. The "peace and love" commune is gone, and owner Rick Klein has reclaimed the adobe compound and 80 acres that he bought in 1967 for $22,000. Klein and his wife, Terry, still cultivate the back-to-the-earth, spiritual atmosphere that made the Buffalo commune a haven for long-haired wanderers 25 years ago, but with one important difference: alcohol, drugs, and tobacco are not welcome. "Our desire," explain the Kleins in their brochure, "is to create a family atmosphere where children are welcome and appreciated and the pursuit of a spiritual practice is nurtured and encouraged."

New Buffalo is still a bit rustic—bathrooms are shared and there are no tubs—but in what other B&B can you drum in a *hogan* or meditate in a *tipi*? You can commune with nature on a sage-covered plain, close the door to your private quarters and snuggle under a down comforter, or read about the "old" Buffalo's colorful history in the Communal Room's sixties-oriented library. A "wholesome, natural foods" breakfast is included in the moderate room tab. And if you really miss that tub, there are several hot springs on the banks of the nearby Río Grande where you can soak in the open (clothing optional) and hearken wistfully back to the flower child era.

If You Go: The **New Buffalo (776-2015)** is in the village of Arroyo Hondo, about 10 miles north of Taos off NM 522.

14 *Best* Place to Commune with D. H. Lawrence

The cremated earthly remains of English novelist D. H. Lawrence are cast in cement on the wooded slopes of his beloved 12,000-foot Lobo Mountain, on a ranch once owned by the writer 15 miles north of Taos.

"Because his life was so sickly and troubled, you can see why Lawrence craved this peaceful setting," says David Dunaway, literary biographer and professor of English at the University of New Mexico. "It's a wonderful place to feel his presence."

In reality, the writer didn't spend very much time here and he died in Europe in 1930. His wife, Frieda, brought his ashes back to the ranch, which was given to the couple by arts patron Mabel Dodge Luhan and later donated to the University of Mexico. The 160-acre parcel is now operated as a retreat and conference center, but is open to the public daily from dawn to dusk. There are picnic tables beneath the cool pines and magnificent views of Taos Valley. Nearby is a cement shrine where D. H.'s ashes and his wife's body are entombed. Many visitors leave personal notes and offerings to the deceased writer, who spent a total of about 18 months here.

If You Go: The **D. H. Lawrence Ranch and Memorial** are at the deadend of a well maintained dirt road. In winter or rainy weather, call ahead for road conditions **(776-2245)**. From Taos, take NM 522 north to San Cristóbal, then follow the signs east about 5 miles past the village.

Insider Tip The serious student of Lawrence will want to examine the large selection of out-of-print D. H. Lawrence titles at the **Taos Book Shop** (New Mexico's oldest), at **122-D Kit Carson Road (758-3733)**. The store specializes in books about Taos and the Southwest.

15 *Best* Wild River

Take the scary tingle of a careening roller-coaster, add the heady thrill of an out-of-control sports car (heading downhill with bad brakes), mix with the adrenaline rush of actual life-threatening danger—topped off by sobering slaps of icewater—and you'll begin to understand what it's like to run whitewater through the **Río Grande Canyon,** a deep gash that cuts through the rugged desert south of Taos.

There is no better way to experience the Río Grande than this. You glide and spin, plunge and recover, through stark and dramatic scenery, set off by steep cliffs and giant boulders. Hawks and ravens circle above, delicate herons and egrets spearfish below. The narrow ribbon of river snakes through it all, whirling and swirling toward the Gulf of Mexico, with you in its merciless maw.

A favorite stretch for rafters is **The Racecourse,** a rocky chute between the villages of Pilar and Rinconada running parallel to US 68. The river is swift and bumpy here, but not particularly dangerous. Well supervised children will have the time of their lives. So will parents—and audacious grandparents.

The best time to go is April through June, when the river is high from snowmelt, but trips are usually available from March through October. You don't need any special skills to take one of these trips, simply the proper footwear, a hat, and sunscreen. The outfitter provides the gear, transport, and, in most cases, a light lunch. Choose between an oar boat—where the guide does all the work—or a paddle raft—where every passenger helps steer through whitewater. For a longer ride through bigger rapids, try **The Taos Box** or **Río Grande Gorge**, both northwest of Taos.

"The Box is the state's best whitewater ride," says Ron Troy, a local river guide who has navigated many trips down the Río Grande and Chama. "I've never been bored on it."

Floating the lower portion of the river takes you to **Embudo Station,** which serves fine food along with its own beer and locally made wine. The restaurant's patio sits on the banks of the river, under beautiful cottonwood trees. Embudo Station is open only during warm-weather months.

If you'd like to forego whitewater altogether, you can descend into the depths of the Río Grande Gorge on foot via the BLM's **Wild and Scenic Rivers Recreation Area,** about 40 miles northwest of Taos near the village of Cerro. Take NM 522 to 6 miles north of Questa, then follow the signs through Cerro to the recreation area. This is indeed one of the wildest areas of New Mexico, with several trails and campgrounds to choose from. The views, especially at sunset, are magnificent.

If You Go: Several experienced local outfitters offer half-day whitewater trips for about $40. You'll pay considerably more to run the Taos Box or Río Grande Gorge. Recommended in Santa Fe are **New Wave Rafting (984-1444), Kokopelli Rafting (983-3734),** and **Southwest Wilderness Center (983-7262)**. In Taos, try **Los Ríos (800 544-1181)** or **Native Sons Adventures (800 753-7559)**. The **Embudo Station's Bar and Restaurant (800 852-4707)** is 25 miles south of Taos and 41 miles north of Santa Fe on US 68.

16 *Best* Rocky Mountain Train Ride

All aboard!

The Toltec & Cumbres Scenic Railroad has an old-fashioned, narrow-gauge steam train that winds its way for 64 miles from the town of Chama through Cumbres Pass and into some of the most gorgeous high-mountain country in New Mexico, eventually depositing passengers in the tiny village of Antonio, Colorado. In the Toltec Gorge, you'll ride through tunnels and across trestles that represent an amazing feat of engineering. You can get on at either end of the line, and ride one-way or round-trip. Forget those cactus-studded images of New Mexico, this part of the state looks and feels more like Yellowstone National Park.

"If you have children or like old trains and great scenery, the Toltec & Cumbres is a marvelous experience," says Josefita Martínez, a native New Mexican whose family members have lived near the railroad for more than a century.

From Memorial Day weekend until mid-October, this is the only time to catch the passenger train on the 64-mile route (the longest and highest of its kind in the United States). It once connected south to Santa Fe and north to Alamosa on a run affectionately called "the chile line." Traveling a different route than nearby roadways, the Toltec & Cumbres also offers half-way trips that stop or start at Osier, Colorado. You can catch a van back to wherever you left your vehicle.

If You Go: Reservations **(756-2151)** should be made well in advance. Prices vary. As this book went to press, the round-trip cost between

Chama and Antonio was $41.50 for adults, $20 for children under 11. For information about tourism in the Chama area, there is a "Welcome Center" at the intersection of US 64 and NM 17 in the center of town. In case you're curious, the train crosses the Colorado–New Mexico state line a total of seven times during the trip. Perhaps that explains why the Toltec & Cumbres is jointly owned and operated by the two states.

17 *Best* Spanish Colonial Church

An old church in Las Tampas.

Santa Fe photographer Sam Adams has spent many years taking pictures of New Mexico churches and has never found one he likes better than the adobe **Church of San José de Gracia** in the tiny Hispano village of Las Trampas.

"The church was built in 1760," Adams explains, "and is lovingly replastered by local residents every year or so. It is an exquisite example of Spanish colonial mission architecture. There are some lovely old paintings inside, too." Hours are irregular, however, and the church is often locked.

Las Trampas is one of the region's oldest European villages and was built in a fortified manner in order to protect its residents during Indian raids. Just north of the community you can see a very old wooden flume that carries irrigation water across an arroyo.

If You Go: **Las Trampas** is 32 miles south of Taos on NM 76 (known locally as the "high road"). The church is easily visible from the roadway.

18 *Best* Family-Style Spa

Ojo Caliente—literally "hot spring" in Spanish—lies on the southern edge of Taos County. The name of both a village and a family-run resort, Ojo Caliente has attracted weary humans for thousands of years. The region's first non-Indian explorer, Álvar Núñez Cabeza de Vaca, came through here in the early 1540s and was surprised to find Apache, Navajo, Ute, Comanche and Pueblo Indians—normally at war with each other—laying down their weapons to peacefully bathe in the healing waters of several natural hot springs.

"They are wonderful waters," wrote Cabeza de Vaca, "bursting out of a mountain."

Visitors relax in one of Ojo Caliente's mineral pools.

Perhaps the Indians knew how special Ojo Caliente was … the only known place in the world where five separate mineral springs flow from what is virtually the same source; They comprise arsenic, lithia, iron, soda, and sodium, varying in temperature from about 90 degrees to almost boiling. Today the complex boasts a small hotel, restaurant, swimming pool, and a combination of private and communal mineral baths. You also can get professional massages, herbal wraps, and mudpack facials, or go horseback riding and hiking in the nearby hills. Attractions include a nearby Anasazi Indian ruin and abandoned mica mines, as well as a historic nineteenth-century round barn.

"This is where *I* go to relax," confesses Denise Cabot, a professional massage therapist from Santa Fe. "It's heavenly."

The spa has been run for many years by the same family, which has kept its rates reasonable. Visitors have access to several natural and manmade pools, plus a Jacuzzi spa. The setting is calming and the staff friendly. The food at the spa's **Poppy's Café** is good or you can drive to nearby restaurants in the village. You can stay in either a small bungalow (with kitchen) or a room in the main lodge (without kitchen).

If You Go: **Ojo Caliente (583-2233)** is 21 miles north of Española on US 285 and 35 miles south of Taos, also via US 285. Bring your bathing suit: wearing one is required.

19 *Best* Artisans' Cooperative

The **Tierra Wools Cooperative Showroom** in the village of Los Ojos has successfully kept alive the area's Spanish colonial weaving tradition as well as its once-thriving sheep industry. Inside a converted general store you'll see local weavers dying and sorting wool yarn, then loading it on looms to be woven into rugs, tapestries, blankets, pillowcases, and so on. There's virtually always someone working at a loom and visitors are welcome to watch and take photos. Of course, you're invited to buy these handcrafted products as well and there's an extensive selection available here.

"There's no question, this is the best place to buy wool textiles in northern Río Arriba County," declares Debora Begel, a journalist and community activist who lives in nearby Ensenada. "The work is of the highest quality and purchase of it keeps traditions and jobs alive in a rural, agrarian economy."

The Tierra Wools enterprise is a venture of a local nonprofit organization called Ganados del Valle ("Livestock of the Valley"), which has worked hard to develop cottage industries that can keep local people meaningfully employed.

If You Go: **Los Ojos** is just west of US 84, about 10 miles south of Chama and 3 miles north of Tierra Amarilla. The **showroom (588-7231),** on the tiny main street of Los Ojos, is open Monday through Saturday from 9:00 A.M. to 6:00 P.M. (May through September), and from 10:00 A.M. to 5:00 P.M. the rest of the year. During the summer, **Tierra Wools** is also open from 11:00 A.M. to 5:00 P.M. Sundays. The town, founded in 1860, has an interesting hybrid architecture that combines New Mexico's traditional adobe walls with steeply-pitched tin roofs and Victorian-era gingerbread trim.

Insider Tip Nearby Tierra Amarilla is the Río Arriba County seat and site of a 1967 armed insurrection involving local activists who claim their lands are still part of Mexico, not the United States. Things have calmed down, but you may still see signs proclaiming land rights sentiments and the Mexican flag still flies in a few places.

20 *Best* Sailing and Windsurfing Lake

Contrary to popular belief, New Mexico is a land of many lakes: more than 200, to be exact. The consensus among sailors and windsurfers is that the best of these is **Heron Lake,** a man-made reservoir created along the headwaters of the Chama River (Willow Creek) and filled by water diverted via an underground tunnel from Colorado's Animas River, as part of a redistribution scheme that is far too complex to explain in this entry.

"The wind conditions at Heron Lake are consistently excellent," reports Marcia Weist, a Las Cruces–based windsurfer who's tried the other major bodies of water in the state. "Watch out for fickle changes in direction in the afternoon, though."

Heron may also be New Mexico's prettiest lake, surrounded as it is by rolling hills of mixed juniper, piñon, and ponderosa forest. "It reminds us of our childhood homes in New England," sighs Cynthia Fulreader, who camps here often with her husband, Gary.

Established in 1972, the 5,900-acre reservoir is a designated "quiet lake," which means motorboats cannot operate above trolling speed. Winds are erratic here, but they tend to be mild, especially in late spring and early summer. Late summer brings sometimes violent afternoon and evening thunderstorms. There are plenty of quiet coves for picnic anchorages and the fishing (for stocked rainbow trout and kokanee salmon) isn't bad either. The water, however, is a bit too cool for most swimmers.

There are a number of campsites along the shoreline, and a 5.5-mile trail winds through the picturesque hills to El Vado, another manmade lake.

If You Go: **Heron Lake State Park (588-7470)** is 10 miles west of Tierra Amarilla via NM 85. Besides picnic tables and restrooms, there is a visitors' center, marina, and boat ramps.

Chapter 4
Albuquerque and Vicinity

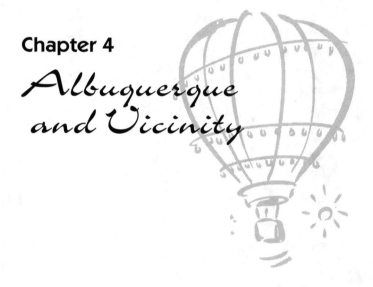

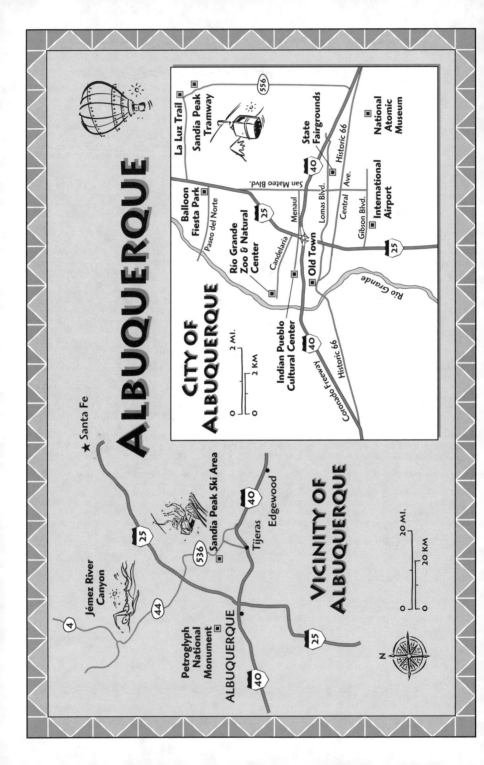

What's Best about Albuquerque

More than one-third of New Mexico's 1.6 million people live in and around Albuquerque, a sprawling, laid-back city that resident novelist Tony Hillerman once observed "has room enough and time."

Yet one thing the state's urban center does *not* have is tourist appeal. Unlike Santa Fe and Taos, which attract visitors by the millions every year with seemingly no effort, Albuquerque is often regarded as an afterthought—a place to go after all the must-see destinations have been seen. Dissatisfied with this second-string image, community activists have put fresh energy into sprucing up and promoting the many attractions and events that make Albuquerque a city that is indeed worthy of a traveler's time and attention.

One characteristic that stands out is the relaxed friendliness of the people who live here. They never seem in too much of a hurry to chat or wave, and they clearly enjoy the company of family and friends.

"There is no pretense about Albuquerque," local writer Mateo Esquibel once observed in *The Alibi* newspaper. "Comfort seems to be woven into the natural fiber of everyday life."

Perhaps it's the dramatic Southwest setting and congenial weather that help Albuquerque retain its small-town charm, even though the population has swelled to more than 500,000. The enormous, crystalline sky is almost always blue and the temperature range is moderate, thanks to a high elevation (5,200 feet) and dry climate (about eight inches of rain a year). There are towering mountain ranges to the north and east, extinct volcanoes and buff-colored plains to the west and south, and the green swath of the Río Grande coursing through the middle. Albuquerque boasts a rich, colorful past and a dynamic, multicultural present. Its pulse is fueled by a diverse and vibrant economy that includes a major university, air force base, and high-tech research center.

Despite its size, Albuquerque is an easy city to get around in. It's divided into four geographic quadrants—NW, SE, SW, and NE—that correspond to the intersecting lines of the north-south railroad and east-west Central Avenue (Albuquerque's main street). When in doubt, remember that the mountains are north and east, while the river and valley are south and west. If you don't have a car, you're in luck: Albuquerque has the best bus system of any New Mexico city.

Our definition of greater Albuquerque includes all of Bernalillo County, plus portions of Sandoval and Valencia counties that encompass the Isleta, Sandía, Jémez, Zia, Santa Ana, and San Felipe Indian pueblos.

There's an intriguing story about the city's name. Spanish immigrants first established an outpost here in 1706, almost a century after Santa Fe was settled. The provincial governor named the village after the official then in charge of the New Spain colonies, the Duke of Alburquerque. This explains why locals affectionately refer to their home town as "The Duke City" and the local baseball team is called "The Dukes." With the coming of the railroad in the 1880s, European-Americans dropped the first "r" in Alburquerque after complaining that the name was too hard for them to pronounce and spell. There's an unofficial campaign led by local writer Rudolfo Anaya to get the missing "r" put back, but officials have shown no interest in complying.

For more information on Albuquerque, please contact the Albuquerque Convention and Visitors Bureau, 20 First Plaza NW, Suite 601, Albuquerque, NM, 87125-6866; or call 800-733-9918; or fax 505-247-9101.

1 Best Place to Realize You're Not in Phoenix

Old Town is exactly that—the "old" Albuquerque. Unfortunately, it's virtually the *only* part of the city that still looks like a sleepy Spanish colonial settlement, with narrow streets, thick-walled adobe buildings, shady portals, and an 18th-century tree-lined plaza. Walking through Old Town, you feel like you could be in Cuernavaca or Seville, but definitely not Phoenix. Or Peoria, for that matter.

"Albuquerque began as a conglomeration of separate agrarian neighborhoods," explains John Knick, an amateur historian and professional tour guide. "You still get a sense of that in Old Town."

This downtown *barrio* was bypassed by developers after 1880, when the railroad was built a couple of miles to the east. Artists and writers rediscovered Old Town in the

The steeples of the San Felipe de Neri Church. Photo courtesy of the Albuquerque Convention and Visitors Bureau.

1930s as a neighborhood of low rent and high character. Few people actually live in Old Town today, though, and most of the homes have been given over to small shops, galleries, and restaurants that cater primarily to tourists. Still, the ambiance is pleasant and the prices are often better than in the trendy boutiques of Santa Fe and Taos. Indian vendors sell their jewelry and pottery (at reasonable prices) along the sidewalks.

On Sundays there's a series of fake **Wild West shoot-outs** on **Romero Street.** If you're lucky enough to visit on a holiday or during a fiesta, you may hear mariachi bands playing outside the historic **San Felipe de Neri Church,** a massive architectural composite in continuous use since 1792. At Christmas time, Old Town is aglow with more than half a million *luminarias* (votive candles inserted in sand-weighted brown paper bags) and San Felipe holds a candlelight mass.

There are many places to eat in Old Town, but arguably the best is **María Teresa,** which occupies a 12-room house built in 1840 and still displays many heirlooms from the Spanish families who lived there over the years. The menu includes both continental and New Mexican dishes, well prepared and moderately priced. Closer to the plaza and also recommended are **La Hacienda** and

La Placita (both on San Felipe). For places to stay, consider the **Sheraton Old Town** or the more intimate **Casa de Sueños B&B,** voted "best B&B" by Crosswinds magazine in 1993.

If You Go: **Old Town** covers several square blocks west of downtown between San Felipe and Romero, and is reached by taking Central Avenue west from I-25 or Río Grande Boulevard south from I-40. Hours of businesses are generally 9:00 A.M. to 6:00 P.M., although many stay open later in the evenings during summer. Street parking is often a problem; you're best off looking for a private or city-operated lot. There's a **visitors' information center (243-3696)** at **305 Romero** where you can pick up tips on what to see in Old Town as well as in the rest of Albuquerque. **Old Town Tours** can be reached at **983-4242. María Teresa (242-3900)** is at **618 Río Grande NW. La Hacienda (243-3131)** at **302 San Felipe NW** and **La Placita (247-2204)** at **208 San Felipe NW.** The **Sheraton Old Town (843-6300)** is at **800 Río Grande NW, Casa de Sueños (247-4560)** at **310 Río Grande NW.**

Insider Tip

The easiest way to learn about Old Town is via a free, hour-long guided tour offered by the nearby **Albuquerque Museum (243-7255).**
Docents explain the history of the community as you roam the barrio's narrow streets. Tours depart from the museum (**2000 Mountain Road NW**) at 11:00 A.M. Wednesday through Friday, and at 1:00 P.M. on Saturday and Sunday.

2 *Best* Place to Realize You're Not in Dallas

Looking for a quick overview of the state's rich Native American heritage? Nothing could be better than the nonprofit **Indian Pueblo Cultural Center,** jointly operated by all 19 of the New Mexico tribes that fall under the Pueblo designation. Besides nicely curated exhibits describing history, language, and culture, you'll find a comprehensive display of arts and crafts from each of the pueblos, accompanied by well produced videos. Among historic tidbits is the fact that the Pueblo Indians started the first civil war in the present-day United States, when they threw out the Spanish in 1680. (Spain reconquered New Mexico in 1692.)

"Our culture is unique," emphasizes Herman Agoyo, past governor of San Juan Pueblo and former chair of the Eight Northern Pueblos Council. "This is the best place to find out what distinguishes our tribes from others."

Artists often are on hand to give demonstrations, and dances are held here daily from May through October (at 11:00 A.M. and 2:00 P.M.) in an outdoor plaza. This is one place where picture-taking of Indian rituals is not only *allowed*, it's *encouraged*. At the center's restaurant you can sample Pueblo food, including posole, meat stew, tamales, and fry bread. The gift shop sells high-quality crafts at fair prices. A small gallery shows contemporary Pueblo art and children can grind whole corn using a traditional *mano* and *metate*.

If You Go: The **Indian Pueblo Cultural Center (800 288-0721)** is north of Old Town at the corner of Indian School Road and **12th Street NW.** Hours are 9:00 A.M. to 5:30 P.M. daily. General admission is $2.50, $1.50 for seniors, $1 for students and children, and free for kids under six.

3 *Best* Place to See a Rattlesnake

See the country's largest public exhibition of rattlesnakes at the **American International Rattlesnake Museum,** established by a former biology teacher who's now dedicated to clearing up misinformation about this much-feared reptile. Founder Bob Myers points out that rattlers do not initiate unprovoked attacks on people—although they will defend themselves when threatened—and their ongoing consumption of rodents and other creatures helps maintain important ecological balances.

"I like this place because the snakes are treated with care and respect," says Clair Tyrpack, a public education specialist for New Mexico's Department of Game and Fish. "There are other places in New Mexico where rattlers are displayed, but often they're mistreated or killed."

The International Rattlesnake Museum. Photo courtesy of the Albuquerque Convention and Visitors Bureau.

There are about 30 varieties of live rattlesnakes here from throughout the hemisphere, including a rare albino and a patternless Western diamondback. Nonvenomous species exhibits include items of Native American medicine and artifacts as old as 15 million years. Videos are used to illustrate rattler behavior.

If you survive the museum experience, you'll be issued a certificate verifying that fact. Don't miss the gift shop on your way out, where *everything* has a rattlesnake theme, from bumper stickers to coffee mugs.

If You Go: The **American International Rattlesnake Museum (242-6569)** is in Old Town at **202 San Felipe Street NW.** Hours are 10:00 A.M. to 6:30 P.M. Admission is $2; $1 for those 16 and under.

4 *Best* Place to See a Bosque

In Spanish, *bosque* means "woodland." In Albuquerque, the word refers specifically to thick stands of trees that shade the fertile bottomland along the Río Grande. According to some sources, these are the largest cottonwood forests on earth. They also comprise of willows, olives, and elms, along with a wide variety of fauna—including beavers, opossums, bats, raccoons, skunks, coyotes, turtles, pheasants, and roadrunners.

Río Grande Nature Center State Park protects a large parcel of bosque in the heart of Albuquerque, an important habitat for migrating waterfowl as well as many resident birds and amphibians.

"You can hike along several miles of riverside trails and tour the amazing visitors' center, which offers a bird's-eye view of the three-acre pond," reports Randy Madsen, a biologist specializing in riparian (river) habitats, home to New Mexico's greatest variety of species. You can often see seasonally migrating snow geese, sandhill cranes, and even an occasional whooping crane, one of the world's rarest birds.

Not far away is the **Río Grande Zoo,** a 60-acre park that is home to more than 1,300 animals from around the world. This zoo is nicer than most, thanks to naturalistic landscaping and spacious cages. During summer, children especially enjoy the petting zoo and special nighttime hours when nocturnal animals can be observed.

"I love to bring my kids to the outdoor concerts," says Rachel Maurer, an Albuquerque mother of two.

The zoo's unusual animals include a snow leopard, Siberian tiger, and several Mexican wolves, a species which, like the jaguar, once roamed southern New Mexico but is now locally extinct. Don't miss the Jungle Habitat building, probably the most humid environment in the entire state.

If You Go: The Río Grande Nature Center State Park (344-7240) is open daily from 10:00 A.M. to 5:00 P.M., at **2901 Candelaria Road NW** (where the road dead-ends). Admission is $1 for adults, 25¢ for children 6 to 12, and free for kids under six. Free tours every Sunday, the **Río Grande Zoo (843-7413)** is open daily from 9:00 a.m. to 5:00 p.m. at **903 Tenth Street NW**. Admission is $4.25 for adults, $2.25 for those over 63 and under 16.

Insider Tip

In early 1997 Albuquerque's new **botanic garden and aquarium** are scheduled to open near Old Town, where Central Avenue deadends at the Río Grande. The complex houses plants from desert and temperate climates as well as 14 large tanks of aquatic life, including a 240,000-gallon shark pool. Admission is $6 for adults, $4 for children.

5 *Best* Place to See a Dinosaur

Albuquerque's **Museum of Natural History and Science** maintains a unique advantage over its competitors in the dinosaur-viewing business. Paleontologists excavating bones on public lands in the state give the museum first crack at whatever remains they find. Since New Mexico boasts one of the largest deposits of dinosaur remains—including the world's biggest species, the aptly named "sizesaur"—there is a continuing supply.

"The museum is a high-tech masterpiece," enthuses Hildy Schwartz, a paleontologist who has excavated many dinosaur bones at a particularly fertile boneyard west of Bernalillo. "Kids can't get enough of the place."

Schwartz's daughter, Mya, joins her mom in riding the Evolator whenever she gets the chance. This video ride is like a time machine geared to take passengers 38 million years back in time to the days when dinosaurs roamed the earth, particularly in the tropical jungles of New Mexico.

"You can explore an ice age cave and stand inside a 'live' volcano," says Schwartz, whose excavations take her as far afield as East Africa. "Mya doesn't have to twist my arm—I love this museum, too." Besides the dinosaur stuff, there's also a "hands-on" educational gallery (where kids can touch real frogs and snakes), a shark tank, and larger-than-life Dynamax movie theater. Call ahead and find out if any new bones have come in: curators will sometimes take you behind the scenes and let you observe the cleaning process.

If You Go: Located at **1801 Mountain Road NW,** the **Museum of Natural History and Science (841-2800)** is open from 9:00 A.M. to 5:00 P.M. daily. Admission is $4 for adults, $3 for seniors and students, $1 for children 3 to 11, and free for those under age 3. There's a separate admission charge to the Dynamax theater. If you happen to stumble across a dinosaur bone, tooth, or egg during your visit to New Mexico, be sure to call the museum's "fossil hot line" at the number listed above.

⌇ 6 *Best* Ancient Indian Art

Petroglyph National Monument may be one of the most peculiar parks administered by the federal government. Created in 1990 to protect thousands of prehistoric Indian rock carvings and drawings from encroaching urbanization, the monument—once in the middle of nowhere—is now virtually surrounded by tract homes, golf courses, and shopping centers.

"It was worth the struggle to preserve this island of land from developers," says the chief of interpretation, Greg Gnesios, noting that there's still a move afoot to build a road straight through the 7,100-acre park. "This rock art remains sacred to the Pueblo people, whose ancestors created it beginning in about A.D. 1300.

Local Indians still worship here, but those events are not open to the public."

Sadly, some non-Indians can not resist the temptation to deface the drawings, or add their own initials to the basalt rocks. Others have cut away large sections of petroglyphs with power saws. Because of shrinking budgets at the National Park Service, patrols are infrequent and few services exist at Petroglyph. There's a small visitors' center, however, and several trails along the nearby escarpment. Here you'll

The "star" petroglyph is one of many interesting pieces of ancient art at Petroglyph National Monument. Photo courtesy of the Albuquerque Convention and Visitors Bureau.

find volcanic boulders covered with a wide variety of striking artwork, including fanciful depictions of birds, mammals, shields, masks, dancers, and natural phenomena, as well as little-understood abstract symbols and designs. Researchers have counted more than 17,000 engraved or encised drawings on these dark boulders, strewn along the 16-mile-long West Mesa below five extinct volcanoes, which you're welcome to climb—they're about 12 miles by car from the visitors' center.

"You'll probably have the place to yourself," says Gnesios. "On an average day less than 100 people visit the park."

Besides the main Mesa Point Trail, there are three other routes through the maze where you can see petroglyphs in a more natural state. Camping is not available but there's a picnic area with restrooms and running water. Remember to bring sunscreen and a hat; the rocks get very warm on a sunny day.

If You Go: **Petroglyph National Monument (839-4429)** is about 3 miles north of I-40 on Albuquerque's west side. Take Unser Boulevard and follow the signs to the visitors' center at **4735 Atrisco Drive NW.** Hours are 8:00 A.M. to 5:00 P.M. daily except major holidays. Admission is free except for Boca Negra Canyon, which costs $2 per car weekends and $1 per car weekdays. Ranger-led tours are offered and trail maps are available at the visitors' center, which also has a small museum and bookstore.

7 Best Tramway

The **Sandía Peak Aerial Tramway** is the world's longest single-span tramway, taking passengers along a 3-mile, half-hour route that gains nearly 4,000 feet in altitude. You're rewarded with an amazing view as the tram glides through four ecological life zones, from a warm high-desert climate to a cool Sandía Mountains pine forest at an elevation of more than 10,300 feet.

"In biological terms, this is like traveling from Mexico to Alaska," notes Albuquerque filmmaker Diana Martínez, a self-described tram fan. "On a clear day, you can see about half of New Mexico from the top."

At the summit is a decent restaurant **(High Finance)**, fun gift shop (that also serves snacks), and the **Sandía Peak Ski Area** (open after Thanksgiving). During summer and fall you can ride a chairlift or mountain bike down the far side of the ridge—during the winter many skiers use the tram to get to the slopes. The most breathtaking time to take the tram is at sunset, when the western sky is aflame with color.

If You Go: The **tramway (298-8518)** is open daily from 9:00 A.M. to 10:00 P.M. except during the second and fourth weeks of April, when it closes for maintenance. Hours vary slightly on holidays and during winter. The cost is $12 for adults, $9 for children and seniors (discounts available if you eat at the **High Finance Restaurant, 243-9742)**. There are picnic areas at both ends of the tramway.

The easiest route to the lower starting point is Tramway Road (NM 556) from I-25 (Exit 234), heading northeast (toward the mountains) for 5 miles to Sandía Heights Road, where you'll make a left. From I-10, take Tramway Road (Exit 167) and head north about 9 miles. For information about skilift rides, call the **Sandía Peak Ski Area** at **298-8518** or **242-9052**.

8 *Best* Hot-Air Balloon Festival

Santa Fe's Richard Abruzzo is coholder of the world's duration record for hot-air ballooning. He and his partner, Troy Bradley, accomplished this in 1992 when their transatlantic crossing veered off course and plopped them down on the sands of western Morocco—six days after takeoff.

Hot-air balloons on the rise at the world's biggest balloon festival. Photo courtesy of Alyssa Pumphrey.

"We expected to come down in some field of clover in Ireland," Abruzzo recalls. "But the winds took us to Africa. Luckily, the nomads who found us spoke English!"

You can get by with English just fine in Albuquerque, too, although dozens of other languages are spoken among the more than 600 balloonists from around the world who gather here for nine days in early October to participate in the world's largest balloon festival—or fiesta, as they say in the Southwest. The **Balloon Fiesta** reportedly has surpassed the Rose Bowl Parade as the most photographed event anywhere. Just ask Kodak, its official sponsor.

Competition begins at Balloon Fiesta Park off I-25, but can be viewed to some degree from all over Albuquerque. Activities include a "key grab" (whoever first reaches a set of car keys set atop a 30-foot pole wins the brand-new automobile they fit), and "special shapes rodeo" (featuring balloons that look like everything from whiskey bottles to peanuts, cows to cartoon figures, soda cans to teapots). Most amazing are the several mass ascensions, in which all participants take off at the same time (usually between 7:00 and 8:00 A.M.), filling the sky with colorful balloons. Also recommended is the Balloon Glow, with synchronized after-dark firings of tethered aircraft. A parade, precision parachute team, and food booths are also part of the fun. Balloon rides are available or you can volunteer to staff one of the many ground crews needed to launch and retrieve the unwieldy aircraft.

So why is the world's biggest balloon festival in New Mexico?

"Flying and observing conditions are excellent here in the fall," explains Abruzzo, whose family not only pilots balloons all over the world but also operates ski resorts near Albuquerque and Santa Fe. "In October, our winds are generally calm; the days are clear and nights are cool.

"Besides the incredible weather," says Abruzzo, "there's plenty of open land that can be used for chasing and landing balloons—although several aircraft seem to wind up in the Río Grande every year. What really makes Albuquerque special for ballooning is an unusual weather phenomenon called 'The Box.' Cool air descends at night from the nearby Sandía and Manzano mountains and flows down the Río Grande drainage. Above this cool river of air are warmer winds, which typically blow from the south and southwest—the opposite direction. This allows pilots to move up and down, backwards and forwards, instead of simply heading off in one direction." So accommodating is The Box, Abruzzo points out, that most pilots can fly for hours above the city and return to the exact point where they took off.

If You Go: The **Balloon Fiesta (821-1000)** is held annually from the first through the second weekends in October. The extravaganza is held at the 77-acre **Balloon Fiesta Park** on the northwest edge of Albuquerque, between Paseo del Norte and Alameda Boulevard NW, about 0.5 mile west of Washington Place. It's best to make room and car rental arrangements far in advance, since many thousands of visitors attend this event. Shuttle buses run between the Balloon Park and all major hotels. One final tip: Dress warmly! Ascensions take place around dawn, and Albuquerque is downright nippy on October mornings. Admission to the launch area is $2. During Fiesta, a tape-recorded summary of events is heard by dialing **243-3696.**

Insider Tip Rides cost about $140 and may only be offered by pilots who carry appropriate insurance. All pilots at the Fiesta are licensed by the FAA and have passed both written and inflight tests. You can book hot-air balloon rides the rest of the year from several firms; call the **Convention and Visitors Bureau** at 842-9918 for a current list.

9 *Best* Place to See an Atomic Bomb

Everything you may want to know about the development of atomic energy—and weaponry—can probably be found within the walls of the **National Atomic Museum.** You can see casings of Fat Man and Little Boy, the bombs dropped in 1945 on Hiroshima and Nagasaki. You can play "nuclear hangman" with a computer, see a video of atomic tests in the Pacific, and read Albert Einstein's letter warning President Franklin Roosevelt about uranium's potential danger. You can even use an electronic gizmo to measure your own radiation exposure. This high-tech museum may seem a little out of place in the post-cold war era, until one realizes that millions of tax dollars are still being spent each year on nuclear bomb research at the nearby Sandía and Los Alamos national labs.

"This place is worth a visit, if only to learn what a pivotal role New Mexico has played in the development of these horrific weapons," says Hugh Gusterson, an anthropologist at M.I.T. and the author of a book about the state's atomic legacy. He points out that there are many peaceful applications of nuclear technology and the exhibits discuss these as well, along with the perennial question of what to do with our deadly nuclear waste.

If You Go: The **National Atomic Museum (845-6670)** is at **Kirtland Air Force Base,** near the Albuquerque Airport. Take Wyoming south (or Gibson east) to K Street SE. As you enter the base, you'll be issued a pass and map to the museum. Look for the B-52 and F-105 bombers parked out front! Open daily (except major holidays) from 9:00 A.M. to 5:00 P.M. Admission is free and tours can be arranged for groups of six or more.

10 *Best* Place to Spend the Night

La Posada is the city's oldest and most elegant hotel. Built in 1939 by New Mexico-born hotelier Conrad Hilton, La Posada combines the luxurious pampering of a bygone era with European-style hospitality and Southwestern architecture. You'll note such typical (and now expensive) regional details as hand-carved corbels, exposed *vigas* (ceiling timbers), mosaic fountains, handmade furniture, Mexican tile floors, and whitewashed walls. The 10-story hotel boasts tastefully appointed rooms and amenities include valet parking, next-door health spa, and a free airport shuttle.

Hilton liked the place so much that he brought his new wife, Zsa Zsa Gabor, here for their honeymoon. His family no longer has ownership, but the lobby-level restaurant—**Conrad's**—commemorates the hotel's founder with delicious food served in an elegant atmosphere. La Posada has flirted with bankruptcy (and possible closure) in recent years so you'd be wise to pay a visit while you can. As Zsa Zsa would say, "It's vunderful, dahling!"

If You Go: La Posada (**800-777-5723** or **242-9090**) is downtown at **125 Second Street NW,** between Copper and Central.

11 *Best* Luminaria Display

In Albuquerque, they're called *luminarias*. In Santa Fe, they're called *farolitos*. This semantic battle has raged for years, with no end in sight. The words translate from Spanish as "little bonfires" and "little lanterns," respectively, and refer to lighted votive candles placed at the bottom of a brown paper bag which, in turn, is anchored by a layer of sand. (To further confuse the issue, Santa Feans use *luminaria* to refer to the welcoming street-corner bonfires they set in their neighborhoods on Christmas Eve.)

"Our New Mexico tradition dates back at least 90 years," says lifelong Old Town resident Juanita Lemus. "It is related to *las posadas*, the ritual in which the search by Mary and Joseph for an inn is reenacted during the nights before Christmas." According to Lemus, the candles illuminate a pathway on the dark streets that the couple can follow, culminating on Christmas Eve with their arrival in Bethlehem for the blessed birth.

If You Go: Although luminarias (many of them now electrically illuminated plastic) are lit all over Albuquerque, Old Town is the best place to see them in their old-fashioned glory: more than 500,000 shine there on the evening of December 24. Tours are available or you can walk through the streets. Private vehicles are discouraged because of the intense traffic congestion. For **Old Town** visitor information: **243-3215.**

12 *Best* Place to Feel Like It's Really New Mexico

Consistently ranked as one of the nation's top state fairs, the **New Mexico State Fair** has something for everyone: rodeos, pie contests, roller coasters, arts and crafts, prize-winning livestock, country music concerts, carnival sideshows, orchid-growing competition, food vendors, dances, exhibits, and much more. A few years ago New Mexican authors even sold their books at a table here. It's the kind of event that is full of surprises, as diverse as the state is big.

Native American dancers at Indian Village, New Mexico State Fair. Photo courtesy of the Albuquerque Convention and Visitors Bureau.

If You Go: Held during the middle two weeks of September, the fair **(265-1791)** takes place at the **State Fairgrounds,** bordered by Central, Lomas, Louisiana, and San Pedro. Open daily from 9:00 A.M. to 11:30 P.M. Ticket prices vary, depending on the day and a visitor's age. Admission is sometimes free during mid-week.

13 *Best* Breakfast

Among locals, the consensus is that **Montoya's Patio Café** in Old Town serves the best breakfast in Albuquerque, although a lot of folks swear by **Grandma's** downtown. Your choice may depend on what you're craving. Montoya's is known for traditional New Mexican dishes like huevos rancheros and breakfast burritos, while Grandma's sticks closer to pancakes, eggs, biscuits, and gravy. **Duran's Central Pharmacy Restaurant** gets the top nod from chile fanatics like Eloy Trujillo: "It's the best I've ever had— even better than what my *abuelita* used to make!" The drugstore diner serves green and red chile in a bowl, without an entrée, or as a condiment on items such as the Torpedo: potatoes, chile, and cheese wrapped in a flour tortilla.

If You Go: Montoya's Patio Café (243-3357) is at 202¹/₂ San Felipe NW. Grandma's (764-8333) is at 318 Central Avenue SW. Duran's (247-4141) is at 1815 Central NW.

14 Best Lunch

Locals also maintain that **Sadie's,** an unpretentious institution that used to be housed in a bowling alley, serves the best *comida típica* in town. This North Valley eatery is known for its huge portions, moderate prices, and hot salsa. Try the green chile stew and pollo guaco (chicken with guacamole sauce). Open Monday through Friday from 11:00 A.M. to 10:00 P.M., and Sunday noon to 9:00 P.M.

The best burritos in town can be found at a take-out stand called **Dos Hermanos,** according to Sharon Niederman, author of *Hellish Relish: Sizzling Salsas and Devilish Dips from the Kitchens of New Mexico*. "Dos Hermanos also serves great tamales and offers enchilada casseroles to take home," noted Niederman in her food column for *Crosswinds* magazine.

Local Mexican restaurant chains with good reputations include **Garduño's** (the original on Fourth Street is a favorite) and **Monroe's** (try their red chile honey on your sopapillas) on Osuna. Another local hangout that gets good marks is **El Pinto,** a huge and venerable restaurant on the city's north side.

If You Go: Sadie's (345-5339) is at 6132 Fourth Street NW. Dos Hermanos (294-8945) is at 2617 Wyoming NE. Garduño's (898-2772) is at 8806 Fourth Street. Monroe's (881-4224) is at 6021 Osuna NE. El Pinto (898-1771) is at 10500 Fourth Street NW.

15 Best Dinner

The **Artichoke Café** is an intimate, unpretentious, and continental place specializing in, as the name implies, luscious artichoke appetizers. Main dishes are inventive and changeable, depending on what's available and how the chef is feeling. He goes organic as much as possible, and all ingredients are fresh—and taste it! An excellent northern Italian restaurant, **Scalo,** has attracted a loyal following for its tasty pasta and fish dishes. The same owner operates **Il Vicino,** an upscale pizzeria that's into gourmet toppings. For that elegant night out, Albuquerqueans flock to **Restaurant André** for its wild game and nouvelle recipes. Chocolate addicts will want to save room for the homemade desserts. For those fixated on the fifties, **The Owl Café** will take you back to the days when formica counters, tuck-and-roll booths, and push-button jukeboxes were the rage. Stupendous chile-decked burgers and French-fried onion rings are the specialty here. For the kind of "power dining" that features rich, classy food in elegant, comfortable surroundings, try **Stephen's,** named one of the top 50 restaurants in the United States by Condé Nast Traveler magazine (beating out every other eatery in New Mexico). Beef and lamb are specialties here, and the service is impeccable.

Construction contractor Paul Steiner says your best bet for authentic New Mexican cuisine is **García's,** which has three locations around the city. For healthier versions of the same dishes (i.e., no lard), try **Tío Tito's.** Local restaurant critic Sally Moore recommends the **May Café** for Vietnamese food ("marvelous soups") and **JR's Bar-B-Q Oyster Bar & Grill** ("especially their brisket"). For fancy dinners a few miles out of town, try **Casa Vieja** and **Desert Rose,** both in the nearby river village of Corrales.

If You Go: The Artichoke Café (243-0200) is at **424 Central SE.** Scalo (255-8782) is at **3500 Central Avenue SE.** Il Vicino (266-7855) is at **3403 Central NE.** Restaurant André (268-5354) is at **1100 San Mateo Boulevard NE.** The Owl Café (291-4900) is at **800 Eubank Boulevard NE,** and Stephen's (842-1773) is at **1311 Tijeras Avenue NW.** García's Kitchen has three locations; try the original at **1736 Central SW (842-0273).** Tío Tito's (883-8486) is at **2017 Menaul NE,** the May Café (265-4448) is at **111 Louisiana SE,** JR's (268-1676) is at **6501 Gibson Boulevard SE,** Casa Vieja (898-7489) is at **4541 Corrales Road,** and Desert Rose (898 2269) is located next door to **Los Colores,** a private weaving museum, **(898-5077)** at **4515 Corrales Road.**

Vicinity of Albuquerque

16 Best Place to Hike Under a Full Moon

Sandía Park Wilderness (during the day). Photo courtesy of Deborah Rich.

Okay, so you've taken the tram up Sandía Crest. For an equally spectacular trip (that burns many more calories), hike the 8-mile **La Luz Trail** from the ridgeline down to Albuquerque. Pick a night when the full moon will be above you for at least four or five hours, since it may easily take that long to descend. Carry a flashlight, food, and water just in case. You'll reach civilization at the **Ellena Gallegos Picnic Area.** There are picnic tables and restrooms at Gallegos, which is also the trailhead for the **Pino Wilderness Trail,** another route to the crest. From the picnic area, it's an easy walk back to the tramway parking lot.

"It's a beautiful hike," say Pat and Jack Songer, who've hiked down La Luz in the moonlight. "And remember, it's all downhill!"

If You Go: For information, call the **Sandía Ranger Station (281-3304)** or **Albuquerque Parks and Recreation (768-3550).** For the route to the tramway parking lot, see the entry in this chapter for "Best Tramway." No mountain bikes allowed and dogs must be on a leash.

17 Best Collection of Carved Miniatures

Ross J. Ward has spent more than 30 years ("while you were watching TV") carving and collecting almost a thousand animated miniature figures from all over the world: enough to create a three-ring circus, frontier village, and turn-of-the-century London at his

Tinkertown Museum. These figurines—most of them capable of mechanical action—average about one-twelfth of real-world size, and include a girl skipping rope, a carnival performer breathing fire, a donkey drinking beer, and a knife-wielding cook chasing a chicken. Other items on display include dozens of wedding-cake figurines and a sailboat that went around the world. Most of this occupies a building constructed out of more than 40,000 empty glass bottles that Ward has cemented together. In an adjacent log cabin is a gift shop where Carla Ward sells collectibles and her own hand-thrown functional pottery.

"I loved it," wrote Jennifer Collins, age 9, in the museum guest registry. "A lot of the toys move around and are really funny!"

"Compulsive," declared actress Bette Midler, who stopped by while making a movie in the area.

"Obsessive," adds the author, who pronounces this monument to eccentricity "a definite must-see."

If You Go: Tinkertown Museum (281-5233) is 1.2 miles north of NM 14 on NM 536 (Sandía Crest Road) in **Sandía Park,** about 20 miles north of Albuquerque. Take NM 14 north via Exit 175 off I-40. Admission $2.50 for adults, $1 for kids; open daily, April through October, 9:00 A.M. to 5:00 P.M.

18 *Best* Bathhouse

Located about 60 miles northwest of Albuquerque in scenic Jémez River Canyon, **Jémez Springs Bathhouse** is an old-fashioned spa dating from the 1870s where you can relax in a soothing, pampered atmosphere. Owned by the village of Jémez Springs and leased to a private operator, the bathhouse offers mineral soaks, outdoor hot tubs, massages, and sweat wraps. The water emerging from the earth here is too hot (168°F) for humans to tolerate, so taps mix cooler water to achieve the desired temperature. The front of this establishment is a retail store featuring hundreds of bath-related items, ranging from foot-rub oils to tub pillows.

There are four other major hot springs in the area, including private pools at the nearby **Zen Mountain Retreat Center** (you must be a registered guest to use these) and three public pools on national forest land north of the village. While en route, stop at Soda Dam along NM 4 to see a geological oddity formed by ongoing low-level volcanic activity.

"The drive north through Jémez Canyon on Hwy 4 has to be one of the most beautiful in New Mexico," says Kate Priest, a Santa Fe-based entrepreneur whose company makes high-energy snacks and personal care products. "My favorite place along the way is Spence Hot Springs, where you can [legally] skinny-dip in rock pools set among pine trees in a peaceful outdoor setting."

If You Go: **Jémez Springs Bathhouse (829-3303)** is in the center of the village, next to a small park. Facilities include separate bathing areas for men and women, and state-licensed massage therapists. **Spence Springs** is a short—but steep—hike east of NM 4, at a turnout located about 7 miles north of Jémez Springs. Look for the National Forest Service signs. If you continue on NM 4 you'll pass through the world's largest *caldera* (volcanic crater), formed when the Jémez Mountains exploded about three million years ago—which explains the region's abundant geothermal activity.

Chapter 5
Central New Mexico

CENTRAL NEW MEXICO

What's Best about Central New Mexico

This is the land that tourists forgot. That's too bad, because central New Mexico has some of the most fascinating attractions in the state. Despite its proximity to Albuquerque, the state's largest city, this region offers remarkable natural wonders and spectacular scenery. Destinations include remote parks and overlooked campgrounds where you may be the only visitor. You can experience quiet Spanish colonial-era villages, traditional Native American pueblos, and small towns that epitomize the American West. While you're here, try the home-style cooking in family-run diners, trace the historic trade routes of early Indians, marvel at the eclectic folk art of "Pop" Shaffer, smell the pine-scented forests, and explore the desolate high desert plains where the humble pinto bean once reigned as king.

Along "old" NM 14—now NM 337—are the old Spanish land grant villages of Chilili, Tajique, Torreón, and Manzano. Still visible in these communities are adobe Catholic churches and crumbling *torreónes*: stone towers used to protect early Hispano settlers from Indian raids. Near the community of Manzano is one of the oldest apple orchards in North America, with fruit-bearing trees from 400-year-old stock. Throughout the region you'll see the decaying remains of farms and ranches homesteaded during the early twentieth century, now abandoned to the elements.

For the purposes of this book, central New Mexico is defined as the area within 70 miles of downtown Albuquerque, but excluding the metropolitan area. This includes portions of Bernalillo, Santa Fe, Torrance, Valencia, Sandoval, and Socorro counties. Communities under this designation include Belén, Socorro, Mountainair, and San Antonio.

1 *Best* Scenic Route between Albuquerque and Santa Fe

"Take the **Turquoise Trail (NM 14)** between Santa Fe and Albuquerque," advises Ty Allison, a professional photographer whose work takes him all through the Land of Enchantment. "The drive north will take a few minutes longer than I-25, but you will get a much better feel for the incredible geographic and cultural diversity of New Mexico."

Begin by following I-40 east from Albuquerque for 15 miles, and pass through Tijeras ("scissors") Canyon, for centuries the gateway to the Río Grande Valley for Plains Indians. There's even an unrestored 80-room, 600-year-old Indian pueblo behind the Tijeras Ranger Station, open daily for self-guided tours.

From the village of Tijeras, follow NM 14 (Exit 175) north along the ridgelines of three mountain groupings: the Sandía, San Pedro, and Ortíz ranges. After passing the bedroom communities of Cedar Crest and Sandía Park, you'll come to the tiny village of Golden (gold, from the first strike in the United States, was once mined here, but garnets are now sought). Worth visiting is the tiny old chapel and nearby general store.

A few miles later you'll encounter the resurrected coal-mining town of Madrid (locally pronounced MÁD-rid), an arts-and-crafts center with an interesting mining museum (kids love it) next to the **Mine Shaft Tavern and Engine House Theater,** where Western melodramas are staged every summer. A virtual ghost town after the mines shut down in the 1940s, Madrid hums with activity today. Check out the old-fashioned soda fountain, boutiques, galleries, and home-style restaurants—you'll find everything from Guatemalan textiles to high-protein buffalo burgers. During warm weather jazz and bluegrass concerts are held in the baseball field at the north end of town. In fall there's an art tour, and during December the whole place is lit up like a Christmas tree.

Several miles past Madrid is Los Cerrillos ("the little hills"), which once boasted 21 saloons to quench the thirst of hardy miners seeking coal, gold, silver, lead, zinc, and turquoise. This sleepy village is now used by movie companies looking for that authentic "Western" look. (If you saw *Lonesome Dove* or *Young Guns,* you saw Cerrillos.) The 21-room **Casa Grande** adobe also offers a petting zoo, B&B, museum, and tours of nearby turquoise mines operated over the centuries by a succession of Pueblo Indians, Spanish colonists, and Anglo pioneers. Also on Main Street, the **What-Not Shop** displays colorful rocks and antiques. Have a cup of ice cream while you browse.

Past Cerrillos, the Trail passes the **Garden of the Gods**—a tall cluster of oddly shaped, 70-million-year-old rocks—before crossing a sprawling arid plain that is slowly filling with the homes of Santa Fe commuters. A favorite eatery along this stretch is the **San Marcos Café,** which serves up fine bluegrass and folk music along with country-style breakfast, lunch, and dinner. Recommended are the San Marcos burrito, green chile lasagna, and bourbon apple pie á la mode.

Back on the road, you'll pass the state penitentiary (with its own adjacent working cattle ranch) and reconnect to I-25 for the short trip into Santa Fe proper.

If You Go: The **Old Coal Mine Museum and Engine House Theater (473-0743)** is on NM 14 in downtown Madrid, adjacent to the **Mine Shaft Tavern.** Melodramas are performed each weekend and holiday from Memorial Day to Labor Day. Admission varies, based on age. Both the **Casa Grande (438-3008)** and the **What-Not Shop (471-2744)** are open daily in downtown Cerrillos. The **San Marcos Café (471-9298)** is a few hundred yards north of the NM 42 turnoff, near the **Lone Butte General Store.**

2 Best Old-Fashioned Farm

"We have a lot of history here," explains Manuela Chávez, making a gross understatement. "What we saved are a lot of things people simply threw away when modern conveniences came along."

Manuela and her husband, Pablo, run the **P&M Farm Museum** as a sideline to their main occupation, growing alfalfa along the Río Grande south of Albuquerque.

"Everything we have is old," Manuela emphasizes, pointing to a beaded red purse that began her collection of antiques. "I have a hard time tossing anything out."

Manuela and Pablo have accumulated many display cases filled with old clothes, dolls, toys, telephones, kitchen utensils, and butter churns. On the grounds outside the crammed rooms are antique cars (including a Ford Model T and Model A from the 1920s), vintage tractors, horse-drawn implements, a sleigh, and a covered wagon that was used as a local "school bus" 60 years ago. Even Manuela and Pablo seem to belong to another time, when people lived at a slower, gentler pace. Their enterprise provides some amazing insights into what rural life in New Mexico was like a generation or two ago.

If You Go: The **P&M Farm Museum (864-8354)** is at **478 Jarales Road**, southeast of Belén. Take Exit 191 off I-25 and follow Main Street north to NM 309, then east to SR 109. The farm itself is south on SR 109 about 2 miles.

3 Best Place to See Hawks and Eagles Close Up

Twice each year since 1985, **HawkWatch International** and the **Western Center for Raptor Conservation** have been recording migrations of birds of prey along the steeply sculpted front range of mountains southeast and northeast of Albuquerque. Eagles, hawks, falcons, ospreys, kestrels, merlins, and other migrating predators are particularly fond of this route, which provides them with plenty of thermal updrafts and food.

Like a canary in a coal mine, a healthy raptor population reflects a healthy environment. Fortunately, the annual counts of scientists and volunteers suggest that the number of raptors in the Rocky Mountain states is on the increase. An average of 3,700 birds are now recorded each season at these sites.

"We're working hard to help us all to better understand the status of each of North America's ecosystems," explains Steve

Hoffman, founder of HawkWatch. "By keeping a count of predatory birds migrating through the Sandía and Manzano mountains we can better understand the condition of various environments."

Visitors, including school groups, are welcome at both banding stations, which are usually staffed in the Sandía Range from February to May and in the Manzano Mountains from August to November.

If You Go: The **Manzano observation area** is near the 9,375-foot summit of Capilla Peak, reached via 9 miles of unpaved U.S. Forest Service road heading northwest from the village of Manzano (42 miles from Albuquerque by NM 337). Follow the Gavilán Trail about 20 minutes to the observation point. There is a campground within walking distance of the site.

The **Sandía site** is reached by taking I-40 east to the Carñuel exit, then heading east on US 66 for 1.8 miles. Turn left into the Monticello subdivision and follow Forest Service Road 522 to the Three Gun Spring trailhead. The observation point is about 2 miles up the FS 194 trail. The hike takes one to two hours each way.

Bring binoculars, sturdy shoes, hat, sunscreen, light jacket, and plenty of water. For dates of observation and site maps, contact **New Mexico HawkWatch (255-7622).**

4 *Best* Goat Petting and Goat Cheese

The tranquil home of Queso de Sánchez **(Sánchez Cheese)** is **Sierra Farms,** a distinctive dairy and cheese factory which offers a free goat-petting area for children. Carmen and Valentín Romero Sánchez are the friendly and enthusiastic owners of this intriguing operation, which has produced delicious goat cheese and goat-milk baked goods since 1976. (Don't miss the chocolate-piñon-ricotta confections!)

Besides 50 or so goats, there are pigs, horses, chickens, dogs, cats, and a fine organic vegetable garden, planted with the help of visiting children every spring. If you make arrangements in advance—and pay a fee—you can milk a mother goat, hand feed her kids from a bottle, and help make goat-milk ice cream during a two-hour tour. During Sunday's afternoon open house (1:00 to 4:00 P.M., March through November) all visitors are welcome to feed the goats, wander around the farm, and use the picnic tables free of charge. Phone ahead to see what special events are planned.

A road sign on the way to Sierra Farms.

These range from Father's Day waffle breakfasts to Halloween pumpkin parties to back-to-school watermelon feeds.

"This is a wonderful place to bring children and have a picnic," declares Michael Oellig, an elementary school teacher who used to raise goats and now brings his students here for the informative tour, lessons on organic farming, and goat petting. "There are always squeals of delight from animals and children alike, but nothing compares to the heartwarming experiences the children have of actually holding baby kid goats while feeding them from a bottle." It brings out the "mother," he says, in both boys and girls.

"And Casa de Sánchez is just as enjoyable for adults," Oellig observes.

If You Go: Sierra Farms (281-5061) is about 17 miles south of Tijeras at the intersection of Cardinal Road and NM 337, just north of the village of Escobosa. Open from 10:00 A.M. to 6:00 P.M. (5:00 P.M. November through February), Tuesday through Sunday, plus some holidays.

5 Best Outdoor Folk Art

Clem "Pop" Shaffer was the sort of energetic entrepreneur that a small, nondescript town like Mountainair is lucky to attract. After moving to "the pinto bean capital of the world" in the early 1900s, this Indiana native was by turns a blacksmith, merchant, horse trader, land speculator, farmer, and philanthropist. But he is best remembered for the humorous and imaginative folk art he created in Mountainair throughout his 84 years.

"Shaffer's hotel and ranch are premier examples of 'folk environmentalist' art," explains Christine Mather, author of *Santa Fe Style* and a former curator at Santa Fe's Museum of International Folk Art. "These are multi-dimensional works that are monumental in scope and constructed over long periods of time, like the Watts Tower of Los Angeles. There is no other folk environmentalist art on the scale of Pop Shaffer's in New Mexico."

The facade of the Shaffer Hotel in downtown Mountainair.

Shaffer's remarkable structures are decorated with playful and elaborate animal figures, human faces, geometric shapes, and Native American symbols (including the "rolling logs" or swastika, used to denote the four seasons, four elements, and four corners of the earth). No one knows exactly what motivated Shaffer to single-handedly create such impressive works, but as an unschooled and technically naive painter/sculptor, he fits the definition of a folk artist.

The Shaffer Hotel was built in 1923 on the site of the Shaffer's original blacksmith shop. Abandoned for most of the previous 40 years, the hotel and dining room (the **Pueblo Café**) was reopened in 1982, but closed again in 1996. By the time you read this, the facility may have reopened. If so, the dining room is worth a visit, even if just for a cup of coffee. The entire ceiling is painted with elaborate Indian designs on cerotex cloth and the eclectic chandeliers are decorated with a fanciful coyote motif. Even the hallway into the kitchen is painted with exotic designs.

Next door, on a shady lot where the Shaffer home once stood, sits an unusual cement wall in which animal and human shapes have been formed with appropriately shaped rocks and shells. Pop Shaffer built the 90-foot fence in 1931.

Rancho Bonito, also on the state and national registries of historic places, was once a working farm that produced fresh food for the hotel's dining room. Here you can see many carvings and structures made by Pop Shaffer in the 1930s and 1940s from pieces of wood and stone. The ranch is owned by the Shaffer family and hours tend to be erratic. If the entrance gate is open, visitors are free to enter and walk around. A small museum contains examples of Pop's art and documents his life story.

If You Go: The **Shaffer Hotel** is near downtown Mountainair on NM 55, one block south of the highway's intersection with US 60. **Pueblo Bonito (847-2832)** is about 300 yards west of NM 55 and 1 mile south of Mountainair. There is no entrance fee. Other attractions in Mountainair include summer rodeos as well as a growing number of artists' studios and galleries.

6 Best Place to Witness a Historic Culture Clash

Salinas National Monument is comprised of three widely-separated Indian ruins that are popularly called "the salt missions" because of their proximity to a large, dry lake bed near the present-day town of Willard that was once an important resource for Indians and Spanish colonists alike. This is one of the most complete regional complexes of 17th-century ruins in the United States.

The layout of Salinas is confusing. It's administered through a National Park Service office in Mountainair, but the actual ruins reside at three separate locations along the eastern flank of the Manzano Mountains, southeast of Albuquerque.

These eroding structures are stark reminders of how the lives of indigenous people were affected by the early Spanish colonizers, who came initially looking for the legendary Seven Gold Cities of Cibola and un-Christian souls to convert. Sadly, these Native American tribes were virtually annihilated by the European invasion and their pueblos were empty by 1680.

The largest of the three sites is **Gran Quivira,** an extensive village of more than 300 gray limestone rooms, six ceremonial kivas, and two Catholic churches. The partially restored structures command a sweeping view of the high desert from a strategic bluff.

"The visitors' center has ancient artifacts on display and videos of varying lengths," explains Juan Gonzales, a National Park

Service ranger at Gran Quivira, who has lived in the area for many years. He has studied the Salinas sites and can tell you how the Tiwa-speaking Indians here traded local salt, corn, piñon nuts, beans, and squash with Plains Indians for buffalo meat, hides, flint, and shells.

Abó is located at a year-round spring on a narrow mountain pass opening into the Río Grande Valley. Its sandstone buttressed **San Gregorio Church,** completed in 1651, is one of the few surviving examples of medieval architecture in the United States. San Gregorio was built alongside an ancient pueblo that is now an unexcavated ruin. A small picnic area rests under tall trees near the Abó spring.

Ruins at Gran Quivara, Salinas National Monument.

The third Salinas unit, **Quarai,** is known for its large, well-restored church, built mostly by Indian women and children between 1626 and 1628. **La Purisima Concepción de Cuarar** has red flagstone walls five feet thick and 40 feet high. This magnificent edifice dominates the valley and is in remarkably good condition, thanks to restoration work done earlier this century. The low mounds nearby harbor unrestored ruins dating from the seventeenth century.

If You Go: No camping is permitted at **Salinas Pueblo Missions National Monument (847-2585)** sites, but picnic facilities, restrooms, and water are available. Camping is available nearby at **Manzano State Park** and various National Forest Service facilities. Each of the Salinas monuments is open daily from 9:00 A.M. to 5:00 P.M. except Christmas and New Year's. **Gran Quivira** is 26 miles south of Mountainair on NM 55. **Abó** is 9 miles west of Mountainair and 0.5 mile north of US 60 on NM 513. **Quarai** is 1 mile west of NM 55 and about 8 miles north of Mountainair. The turnoff is at the village of Punta de Agua. The area's best restaurant is the **Willard Cantina (384-9216)** in the village of **Willard,** 14 miles east of Mountainair on US 60. Try the stuffed sopapilla with red chile.

7 *Best* Glow-in-the-Dark Rocks

In Socorro, the **Mineral Museum at the New Mexico Bureau of Mines** is a Shangri-la for anyone interested in unusual rocks, such as those that shine brilliant colors when exposed to ultraviolet ("black") light. More than 10,000 specimens are on display here, including a large number of fossilized plants and animals as well as crystals, fossils, and dinosaur bones. You can even buy a set of New Mexico minerals in the gift shop.

"This is the best place to see the kinds of rocks that underlie New Mexico," says Mark Seymour, a chemical physicist who graduated from New Mexico Technical University, formerly the New Mexico School of Mines. "The collection is very comprehensive and includes samples from all over the world."

If You Go: The **Mineral Museum (835-5420)** is located on **School of Mines Road** in the **New Workman Center,** a building on the New Mexico Technical University campus. Open weekdays from 8:00 A.M. to 5:00 P.M. Admission is free.

8 *Best* Early-Bird B&B

For comfortable overnight accommodations that assure you easy access to our feathered friends, Santa Fe-based writer Peggy van Hulsteyn recommends the **Colonel Eaton House** in Socorro, a 100+-year-old home with five guest rooms (each with private bath).

"Bird pictures and Audubon books are at every turn," says Van Hulsteyn, author of *The Birders' Guide to Bed-and-Breakfasts.* "This is a bird-lover's nest."

With her binoculars and personal field checklist, owner Anna Appleby certainly looks the part of a true aficionado. "Birding makes the world more beautiful," she explains.

Guests who are eager to greet the bosque's birds at sunrise can pack along one of Appleby's Early Birder baskets: a thermos of hot coffee, chocolate, or tea, and fresh pastries. A bountiful full breakfast will be ready upon their return to the Eaton House. This Victorian mansion, by the way, is a registered state historical building.

For dinner, try the historic **Val Verde Steakhouse,** which specializes in (you guessed it) beef entrées. It's in an old hotel building, built in 1919 in the then-popular Mission revival style. The nearby **El Sombrero** offers good Mexican food.

A runner-up in the bosque B&B category is the **Casa Blanca B&B** in San Antonio, 8 miles north of the reserve. Phoebe Wood has renovated the 1880s adobe farmhouse, which has two sitting rooms, a large veranda, and wood-burning stoves in both double-bed guest rooms. The Casa Blanca is closed during the summer months.

One of many Victorian homes in Socorro.

If You Go: Socorro is about 15 miles north of the Bosque del Apache on I-25 (75 miles south of Albuquerque). **Eaton House (800-383-CRANE or 835-1067)** is at **403 Eaton Avenue.** The **Val Verde Steak House (835-3380)** is at **203 East Manzanares Street** and **El Sombrero** is on the plaza. **Casa Blanca B&B (835-3027)** is at **13 Montoya Street** in San Antonio.

9 *Best* Place to See a Whooping Crane

The **Bosque del Apache National Wildlife Refuge** (the name means "riverside forest of the Apache") protects one of the Southwest's most important habitats for tens of thousands of migrating birds, as well as a large resident population of ducks, herons, and other waterfowl. A few extremely rare, six-foot-tall whooping cranes fly here from Idaho to spend the winter, along with huge numbers of snow geese and sandhill cranes from the upper Midwest and Canada. Scientists have been trying to bolster the population of Idaho/New Mexico whoopers by integrating them with the sandhills, with little success. Only about 200 whooping cranes exist, and the only other flock shuttles along a busy corridor between Canada and south Texas.

"I think this is the most spectacular waterbird refuge in the country," contends Phil Norton, the Texas transplant who manages the refuge for the U.S. Department of Agriculture. He notes that regular visitors have included the late Roger Tory Peterson, renowned bird-guide author and illustrator, as well as Pete Dunn and Ken Kaufman, contributing editors of *American Birder* magazine. Jazz flute player Herbie Mann and mystery novelist Judith van Gieson—both New Mexico residents—say they love coming here, too.

A sandhill crane (center) at Bosque del Apache Wildlife Refuge.

"The Bosque del Apache is a premium place for birders," says Ken Hollinga, an American Birding Association official. "As a major wintering area for waterfowl, it's of national significance. You'll see lots of raptors and land birds as well."

Take advantage of a 12-mile, self-guided auto tour through the 57,000-acre refuge and you can see peregrine falcons, bald eagles, swans, Canada geese, mallards, wild turkeys and more than 300 other bird species, along with coyotes, bobcats, porcupines, deer and other mammals. Use the observation towers and binoculars for a better look.

If You Go: The **Bosque del Apache (835-1828)** begins 8 miles south of San Antonio (93 miles south of Albuquerque and about 20 miles south of Socorro) along a quiet stretch of the Río Grande on NM 380 (US 85), which runs on a north-south parallel to I-25. Visitors' center hours are 7:30 A.M. to 4:00 P.M. weekdays and 8:00 A.M. to 4:30 P.M. weekends, but you can drive the auto loop tour from one hour before sunrise to one hour after sunset. Admission is $2 per vehicle. Overnight visitors are not allowed. The visitors' center posts a count of bird species in residence and you can listen to tape-recorded calls that may help you identify various birds.

The best time to go is winter, when the bird population soars to the hundreds of thousands, or the weekend before Thanksgiving each November, when the **Bosque Fall Festival** celebrates the return of cranes and snow geese to what is widely regarded as the Southwest's premiere winter bird sanctuary. The event—cosponsored by the City of Socorro, the local Lion's Club, and the Socorro Chamber of Commerce—includes a wildlife photography workshop, pancake breakfast, birding lectures, history programs, and tours of the refuge (and other area destinations) by area experts.

10 *Best* Chile Cheeseburger

Adolph and Rowena Baca's **Owl Bar & Café,** in the farming village of San Antonio, has been serving its famous green chile cheeseburgers since 1945, when hungry nuclear scientists from Los Alamos began stopping in after a hard day tinkering with atomic bombs at the nearby White Sands Missile Range.

"Somebody had said to me, 'Don't miss the green chile cheeseburger at the Owl Bar,'" former CBS-TV correspondent Charles Kuralt noted in his 1995 book, *America*. "Unlike most of the food tips I've collected on the road, this proved to be admirable advice."

The Owl's beer tastes as good as its burgers, Kuralt points out, adding that the immense hardwood bar came from a five-room boarding house that stood nearby until the 1940s. It was operated by a local man named A. H. "Gus" Hilton, father of Conrad. The humble structure was the first Hilton Hotel and, literally, where Conrad got his start in the business—as a baggage handler.

While waiting for your cheeseburger, check out the vintage photos of weapons testing at the nearby White Sands Missile Range (San Antonio is close enough to feel and hear the explosions) or scan the seemingly unending collection of owls.

Runners-up: On Sundays, when the Owl is closed, try **Manny's Buckhorn Bar** across the street. There's also a fine **Owl Café**

(291-4900) 800 Eubank NE, Albuquerque, that's associated with
the San Antonio restaurant, but purists insist on the original.

If You Go: The Owl Bar and Café (835-9946) is open daily except
Sunday from 8:00 A.M. to 9:30 P.M. at the intersection of NM 1 and NM
380.

Insider Tip For non-New Mexicans, it should be reiterated
that chile refers to the spicy red or green
peppers that are an essential element of local
cuisine, chili is the meat-and-bean stew in which
chile makes a guest appearance.

11 *Best* Arms Race Encounter

Twice a year—on the first Saturdays of April and October—the
public is invited to participate in a government-guided tour of
the desolate place where the atomic age was born on July 16, 1945.
For the other 363 days of the year, **Trinity Site** is strictly off-limits. Located in the 4,000-square-mile **White Sands Missile Range,**
the location is still vulnerable to armed forces weapons testing,
much of it top secret. You can see where the experimental A-bomb
built by Los Alamos Laboratories was detonated from the top of
a 100-foot steel tower. Other than some man-made rubble, a monument, and sand fused by the heat, there's not a lot here. Most artifacts were removed 50 years ago by military officials.

"So bright was the early-morning flash, that witnesses claim
to have seen it as far away as El Paso and Santa Fe, more than 200
miles distant," recalls Pedro Castellano, who worked at Los
Alamos Labs in the late 1940s. "Windows shattered in Silver City,
120 miles to the west."

An intentionally misleading story was distributed by authorities to local newspapers, falsely attributing the explosion to non-
military activities. Only later did the public learn that the Trinity
blast was the final (and decisive) test before President Truman
ordered the atomic bombing of Japan in an attempt to bring World
War II to a speedy conclusion.

If You Go: **Trinity Site** is about 20 miles directly south of the tiny community of Bingham (12 miles southeast of San Antonio), via US 380. You can drive unescorted to the site through Stallion Gate between 8:00 A.M. and 2:00 P.M. The army also runs buses to the **McDonald Ranch,** about 2 miles away, where final assembly of the bomb took place. Information: **678-1134.**

Chapter 6

Northwestern New Mexico

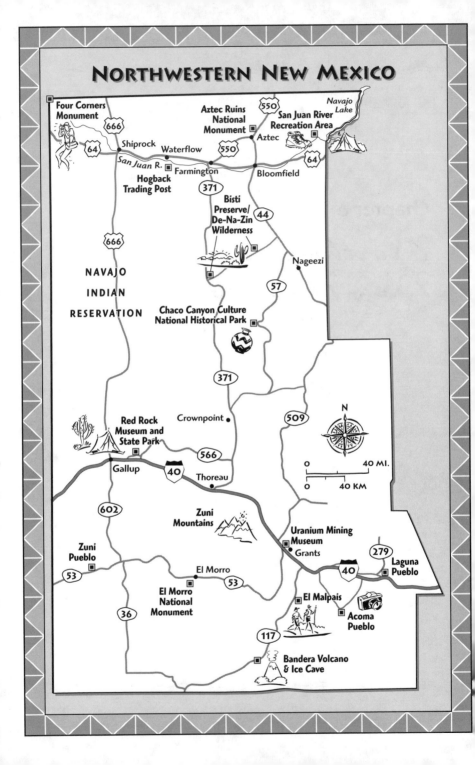

What's Best about Northwestern New Mexico

This is classic New Mexico, as viewed by the outside world. You've seen it a hundred times on the movie screen: the puffy-cloud skies, wide plains, tall mesas, and rocky canyons. Stunning vistas are evident particularly around the Four Corners, where the borders of New Mexico, Colorado, Arizona, and Utah come together.

Much of this high-desert region is occupied by the Navajo Nation, the largest and most populous Indian reservation in the United States. The area is the traditional homeland for members of other tribes as well, including the Jicarilla Apache, Mountain Ute, Zuni, Ácoma, and Laguna. Hispanos, African-Americans, Asians, and Anglos also have been an important part of the cultural mix here for many years.

But before all of these "newcomers," northwestern New Mexico was the domain of the Anasazi people, who prevailed from about A.D. 100 to A.D. 1200. Anasazi is a Navajo word that loosely translates as "our ancient enemy." Because of the pejorative nature of this term, the Anasazi are now often referred to as "the ancestral Pueblo people," although it's not clear what became of them. Somehow these enterprising Native Americans managed to farm, hunt, build, and thrive in an unforgiving environment. The Anasazi built great cities that displayed a masterful knowledge of stone-masonry and dryland farming. They apparently learned many agricultural techniques from Mexico's Toltecs, who traded with them from the far south.

A profound understanding of astronomy is also evident in the layout and orientation of many Anasazi ceremonial structures. By the late twelfth century, following a severe drought, these communities were almost completely abandoned. Archaeologists are still trying to piece together likely reasons for this, although many experts believe that the descendants of the Anasazi migrated to wetter areas and became the Pueblo and Hopi people of Arizona and New Mexico.

Distances are vast in this sparsely populated area and nature displays her prowess on a grand scale. A giant lava plug west of Farmington, for example, rises more than 1,700 feet above the surrounding plain. The aptly named Shiprock monolith is a stunning landmark for hundreds of square miles. Not far away, the Bistí Badlands are a harsh labyrinth of oddly shaped and grotesquely eroded formations that seem better suited to another planet. Hovering above it all, near Grants, is lofty Mount Taylor, a dormant volcano that is sacred to the area's native people and cloaked much of the year with snow.

You'll need your own vehicle to see this part of the state adequately. Public transportation is very limited and does not serve most of the destinations in this chapter. Because of the region's temperature extremes—hot in summer, cold in winter—it's best to visit the area in spring or fall.

For the purposes of this book, northwestern New Mexico is defined as all of San Juan, McKinley, and Cibola counties, plus portions of Sandoval and Río Arriba counties. Communities within this designation include Gallup, Farmington, Aztec, Bloomfield, Grants, Zuni, Dulce, Crownpoint, and Cuba.

1 *Best* Place to Be in Four States at the Same Time

Okay, okay, so it's the *only* place you can be in four states at the same time. That's all this spot has going for it, but why miss an opportunity? You'll find a cement slab at the exact spot where New Mexico, Utah, Arizona, and Colorado come together. Visitors, one after another, contort themselves in order to place different parts of their bodies in each state simultaneously. (A scaffolding is provided for easy picture taking.)

"I did it with four fingers," reports Rachel Goodwin, age six. "It felt kinda silly."

Yes, it may feel silly, but as long as you're there you might as well shop. Dozens of Navajo vendors offer jewelry, pottery, and other items at the many stalls that surround the monument. Drinks and snacks are on sale, too.

If You Go: Coming from New Mexico, the **Four Corners Monument** (located on the Navajo Reservation) can be approached via two routes. From Shiprock, the nearest town of any size, take US 666 north for 21 miles (into Colorado), then head west for 17 miles on US 160. The quicker alternative is to take US 64 west from Shiprock for 24 miles to Teec Nos Pos, Arizona, then head north for 6 miles on US 160. There's no admission charge and the monument is open around the clock.

2 *Best* Trading Post

For more than a century, trading posts have served as a vital symbiotic meeting ground for Navajo and Anglo cultures. This is where the Navajo (who call themselves Diné) have long bartered their piñon nuts, handwoven rugs, silver jewelry, mutton, and wool for dry goods, tools, and farm supplies sold by non-Native merchants. Most Indians drive pickups now instead of horse-drawn wagons and their one-stop shopping centers are gradually being supplanted by Wal-Marts and Thriftiways, yet many posts still operate much as they did 100 years ago.

"The best of these old-style stores is the **Hogback Trading Company**," says Fred Harrison, Jr., a Navajo contractor who lives in nearby Shiprock. He's referring to a 10,000-square-foot, two-story emporium that sells authentic, high-quality collectibles, including rugs, baskets, pottery, jewelry, and even Hopi kachinas. The original store, now a ruin across the highway, was built by the Wheeler family in 1871. The Hogback is the oldest trading post serving the Navajo Nation, which begins at the parking lot.

Nearby Waterflow is also home to **Bob French Navajo Rugs,** one of the state's largest purveyors of handwoven textiles. **Carson's** is another fine example of a trading post from an earlier era. Built on the edge of Navajoland in 1916 by sheep rancher Stokes Carson, the business has changed owners but still does a thriving business.

Chaco Canyon visitors may want to stop by the well-stocked **Nageezi Trading Post,** northeast of the national park. Rugs, jewelry, and other Navajo-made are sold, along with groceries and soft drinks. Overnight accommodations are available here at the **Inn At The Post B&B.**

If You Go: The **Hogback Trading Post (598-5154)** is near Waterflow, 6 miles east of Shiprock and 15 miles west of Farmington on US 64. It's open Monday through Saturday from 8:00 A.M. to 5:00 P.M. **Bob French's Navajo Rugs** can be reached at **598-5621. Carson's (325-3914)** is 20 miles south of Bloomfield on San Juan County Road 7150. Open daily except Saturday. The **Nageezi Trading Post and B&B (632-3646)** is on NM 44 at NM 57, about 20 miles north of Chaco Canyon.

3 *Best* High School Baseball Championship

Are you a baseball fan who's fed up with the highfalutin major leagues? You can see the very best teams from U.S. high schools compete in Farmington early each August during the **Connie Mack World Series Baseball Tournament.** The weeklong event involves 17 games played at 4,000-seat Ricketts Park, one of the best amateur ballparks in the country.

"Lots of scouts are on hand from college and professional teams, and there's always plenty of promising young talent for them to choose from," says Tito Griego, a retired scout who lives in Farmington.

There are lots of motel rooms and restaurants in Farmington, most of them adequate but none impressive. This is a no-nonsense, hardworking town, largely dependent on agriculture (three rivers converge here) and the oil industry. A worthy attraction is the **Farmington Historical Museum**, which has an interesting hands-on exhibit for children and a replica of the turn-of-the-century business district of Farming Town, as it was once known.

If You Go: To find out more about the **baseball tournament,** call **599-1184.** The **Farmington Historical Museum (327-7701)** is free and open Tuesday through Friday from noon to 5:00 P.M., 10:00 A.M. to 5:00 P.M. on Saturdays, at **302 North Orchard.**

4 *Best* Kiva with Farolitos

Early New Mexico explorers were confused about who was responsible for the impressive stone structures they stumbled upon near the Animas River. Thinking no local Indians could possibly have been sophisticated enough to build the three-story complex they beheld, the Europeans labeled them "Aztec ruins." But the Aztecs of central Mexico never came here and, in any event, flourished hundreds of years *after* these buildings were erected. Archaeologists now know that this was an outpost of the region's Anasazi civilization.

The Great Kiva at the Aztec Ruins National Monument.

This misnamed **Aztec Ruins National Monument** encompasses three acres of ruins, including about 400 rooms. A special attraction here is the "great kiva," a huge underground ceremonial chamber that was one of the most sacred spaces in the Anasazi culture.

"This is among the largest fully restored kivas anywhere," says Tom Windes, a staff archaeologist for the National Park Service. "It's 48 feet in diameter and has a roof weighing 90 tons. The wooden vigas were made from pine beams hand carried from many miles away. Imagine building this without the benefit of pack animals or metal tools."

In the days leading up to Christmas each year, thousands of farolitos (candlelit lanterns made of sand-filled paper bags) are placed on the walls of the kiva and the surrounding ruins for a subtle but stunning visual effect.

The adjacent town of Aztec's Main Street boasts a variety of architectural styles, represented by more than 75 buildings on historical registers. The well curated **Aztec Museum** has exhibits pertaining to human settlement of the area and arranges walking tours of the historic district.

If you like ancient Indian history, consider a side trip to the 700-room **Salmon Ruin,** an impressive Chaco outlier similar to

Aztec, situated between Bloomfield and Farmington. The C-shaped structure is named after a homesteader who voluntarily protected these Anasazi artifacts from modern vandals and pot hunters—although the Mesa Verde Indians ransacked the place centuries ago. Guides will show children how to throw the *atlatl*, a dartlike weapon used by the Anasazi for hunting before the bow and arrow were developed. You'll find a gift shop, museum, and **Heritage Park,** which displays life-size replicas of Navajo, Ute, and Apache dwellings.

Ruins at Aztec National Monument.

If You Go: Aztec National Monument (334-6174) is about 1 mile north of Aztec and a few blocks off US 550, the main road to Farmington. Open daily from 8:00 A.M. to 5:00 P.M., until 6:30 P.M. June through August. Admission is $3 per car. The **Aztec Museum (334-9829)** is open daily (except Sunday) from 9:00 A.M. to 4:00 P.M. at **125 Main Street.** Salmon Ruin (632-2013) is 12 miles southwest of Aztec between Bloomfield and Farmington on US 64. It's open daily from 9:00 A.M. to 5:00 P.M. Admission is $1 for adults, 50¢ for kids under 16.

5 *Best* Fly-Fishing

You'll find terrific fly-fishing streams throughout New Mexico, but the **San Juan River Recreation Area** immediately downstream from Navajo Lake is known throughout the world as a premiere casting spot, with the first 3 miles below Navajo Dam reserved exclusively for anglers. You can try your skill at landing several species of trout, with a good percentage likely to exceed 20 inches in length. By law, in fact, along this stretch of the San Juan anything smaller must be tossed back. You'll find plenty of paved trails and wooden fishing platforms along the embankment for your convenience.

"Like the ocean," angler David Gómez wrote in *New Mexico* magazine, "the San Juan [has] its siren call: a certain mystique based on big, wily trout used to the presence of humans, tiny flies, and year-round fishing."

The San Juan is an excellent 12-month stream, while the Río Grande, Pecos, Jémez, and Chama rivers of north-central New Mexico are better suited to fall fly-fishing.

If You Go: The **San Juan River Recreation Area (632-1770)** is about 17 miles east of Aztec via NM 511 or NM 173, between Cottonwood Campground and Navajo Dam, which forms the third-largest lake in New Mexico (stocked with trout, salmon, bass, catfish, and crappie). For a list of local outfitters and guides, call **Farmington's Visitors and Convention Bureau** at **325-0279.** For information on licensing, limits, and locations, contact the state's **Department of Game and Fish** at **800-ASK-FISH.**

6 *Best* Bizarre Landscape

The isolated **Bistí** (pronounced "bist-EYE") and **De-Na-Zin wilderness areas** are located on Bureau of Land Management acreage southeast of Farmington. You'll see wind-sculpted clay and sandstone mesas, spires, and "hoodoos" (mushroom- and phallus-shaped stone monuments) naturally dyed by peculiar green, blue, red, and orange pigments. The large "caps" balanced atop these tall columns are harder rocks that have better resisted erosion over the millennia.

Within the 30,000-acre Bistí preserve are tens of thousands of fossilized animals and petrified plants, including stone tree trunks up to 50 feet long. They're reminders of a time when New Mexico was covered by lush tropical forests and inhabited by huge dinosaurs. All told, more than 200 species of plants and animals have been identified in the Bistí Badlands, including giant tree ferns and fierce tyrannosaurs. The rich biological environment of the past is a stark contrast to the dry, forbidding landscape of the present. Of course, were it not for the large number of dinosaurs and other critters roaming through lush forests here 65 million years ago, there would be no oil and gas industry in northwest New Mexico today, since petroleum products are the residue of their decayed bodies.

"It's a weird, wild place; unlike any we've ever been in," says Donna Henry, a naturalist who likes to explore the area with her geologist husband, Doug. "This is inspiring solitude at its best." The Henrys advise that there are no established trails here and it's easy to get lost. Bring a companion!

The nearby De-Na-Zin ("tall crane") Wilderness is an eerily empty landscape suited for hikers who are even more adventurous.

Don't disturb the formations at either site: all are protected by federal law. Both preserves were created, incidentally, after environmentalists protested a proposed strip-mine operation in the area.

If You Go: For information, call the **BLM Farmington Resource Area Office** at **599-8900.** Avoid the area during times of high temperatures or intense rainfall. Bring sunscreen, a hat, and drinking water. The **Bistí** parking lot and (primitive) campground is about a mile east of NM 371, about 36 miles south of Farmington and 75 miles north of Thoreau. To get to Bistí's main entrance, follow the signs on a gravel road past the (now closed) Gateway Mine. **De-Na-Zin** is about 15 miles east of the Bistí parking lot on San Juan County Road 7500: watch for a sign marking the dirt road to the entrance.

7 *Best* Place to Learn about the Anasazi

The Anasazi Indians reached the peak of their remarkable civilization in a wide, bleak valley called Chaco Canyon—unknown to Westerners until the late nineteenth century. At its height in A.D. 1000, this was one of the largest cities in temperate North America and today it is unquestionably New Mexico's most impressive archaeological monument. The site, now federally protected, is in a remote area roughly 200 miles northwest of both

Santa Fe and Albuquerque. It is 60 miles from Farmington, the nearest town of significance.

Chaco Canyon Culture National Historical Park preserves and displays what some archaeologists have labeled "America's Stonehenge," a reference to the many sacred structures and monuments that were erected here in a precise relationship with the sun, stars, and particular celestial events such as solstices and equinoxes.

"Construction began on the edges of the canyon in about A.D. 700 and continued for about five and one-half centuries," explains Steve Lekson, president of Crow Canyon Archaeological Center and the author of several books about Chaco. "The artifacts found at Chaco Canyon suggest that this was a religious, trading, and governmental center, the capital of a sophisticated civilization that eventually spread itself over hundreds of square miles of what is now New Mexico, Arizona, Utah, and Colorado."

A view from the sandstone cliffs near the Pueblo Bonito ruins at Chaco Canyon.

There are 13 major Anasazi ruins here, along with more than 400 smaller sites spread along the banks of an ephemeral stream that winds between widely separated sandstone walls. Many ruins contain ceremonial kivas that show precise astronomical alignments. Not to be missed is **Pueblo Bonito,** a three-story complex at the base of a sheer sandstone cliff, and **Casa Rinconada,** with Chaco's best-preserved kiva.

Early residents of Chaco Canyon constructed an amazing 1,200-mile network of arrow-straight roads, most easily visible from the air. Like many things here, their exact purpose remains unknown, although they may have been used to roll ponderosa pine logs from faraway mountains.

Although it's easy to see much of Chaco in a single day, the experience is much more profound if you can spend at least one night here, soaking in the delicate beauty, listening to the deafening silence, and meditating on the fate of the Anasazi. Especially recommended is a hike to an outlier ruin, such as **Pueblo Alto** or **Tsin Kletsin.** By taking your time to really see and feel Chaco's presence, you'll better understand why the United Nations has declared this a World Heritage Site, ranking it among Egypt's Great Pyramids and Mexico's Chichén Itzá.

The Wijiji Ruins at Chaco Canyon.

If You Go: From the north, take NM 57 south from NM 44 on 26 miles of unpaved road. (There are NM 44 turnoffs at both the Blanco and Nageezi trading posts.) From the south, head north from Crownpoint for 36 miles on NM 57/197. (Take the NM 371/57 exit 5 miles east of Thoreau off I-40 and head north to Crownpoint.) The route from Nageezi to Chaco is easiest. **Gallo Campground** is near the visitors' center. Otherwise, the closest accommodations (with the exception of a few rooms at **Nageezi Trading Post and B&B, 632-3646**) are in the Farmington or Grants areas, about two hours in either direction by car. Note that Chaco's single campground fills up early, sometimes by 3:00 p.m. on weekends. You should also know that off-trail hiking and bicycling are forbidden, due to the fragile nature of the ruins. You can get water at the Chaco visitors' center (which also has an excellent video presentation) but no other services are available. Avoid the hot and rainy months when visiting. Information, including road conditions: **786-7014** or **988-6727.**

8 *Best* Rug Auction

It's a scene straight out of a Tony Hillerman novel: a hundred solemn Navajo women sit, arms folded, on plastic benches in the back of the Crownpoint Elementary School gym while a fast-talking cowboy in a 10-gallon Stetson auctions their handsome handmade rugs to eager Anglo buyers crowded around a platform piled shoulder-high with colorful textiles. Gasps of admiration fill the room when a particularly elegant tapestry is held up for display— and fierce competition may push the bidding past $3,000 in the blink of an eye. Meanwhile, along adjacent hallways, Indian entrepreneurs sell silver jewelry, wooden kachinas, bags of piñon nuts, and steamy cups of mutton stew.

In a cross-cultural ritual that merges visionary form with mercenary function, the drab village of Crownpoint blooms like a desert flower during its auctions of colorful woolen rugs, a vital ingredient in tribal commerce since the late nineteenth century. The **Crownpoint Rug Weavers Association** oversees the sale of hundreds of member-made rugs on (usually) the third Friday night of every month beginning at 7:00 P.M., with merchandise on display in the school gym beginning at 3:00 P.M. Astute buyers examine rugs in advance, checking for symmetry, curling, fabric, and design.

"The sale is truly a cultural adventure," says Colleen Tsosie, a Navajo educator who believes the Crownpoint Rug Auction offers one of the best ways to learn about modern Navajo life.

Auction prices, selection, and artistry are excellent—with many weavings of museum quality.

"Whether the weaving is old or new, be informed and buy what you love," advises Kathleen Sandrin, a weaver and former textile restorer of Navajo rugs. "Don't get seduced by what appears to be a 'great deal.'"

If You Go: Crownpoint is 34 miles north of I-40 on NM 371 (NM 57 on some maps). The village has no overnight accommodations: closest motels are in Grants, about an hour south. For auction details, call the **Weavers' Association** at **786-5302**.

9 *Best* Indian-Majority City

Named after one of its founding railroad workers, Gallup has been an important Southwest crossroads for more than a century. Coast-to-coast trains stopped here to take on coal and water, while entrepreneurs operated trading posts and general stores that served residents of the nearby Indian reservations. When Route 66 (now called Hwy 66 Avenue) came through in the 1920s, many highway travelers found this an ideal place to eat a meal, spend the night, and buy Native American trade goods. Later, many people in the area were hired as uranium miners. Today, a diverse economy keeps Gallup humming. Although it's not actually on a reservation, it has the highest percentage of Native American residents of any sizable town in New Mexico.

"As an Anglo, I learned for the first time what it feels like to be a minority," says Barton Smith, a former trader of Indian goods, recalling the years he lived in Gallup. "The place feels truly multicultural, which I like."

Many historical buildings remain in Gallup and these are pointed out during walking tours of the city each May during **New Mexican Heritage Preservation Week.** You can see them on your own, of course. Noteworthy structures include the **Harvey Hotel** at **408 West Coal Avenue,** the **Grand Hotel** at **306 West Coal Avenue,** and the **old train station downtown.**

The best place to stay is the **El Rancho Hotel,** built in 1937 by the brother of movie director D. W. Griffith as a hangout for the many stars who did location work near Gallup in the 1930s and 1940s. Each room is named after a famous actor or actress who stayed there, including Ronald Reagan, Katharine Hepburn, Burt Lancaster, and Gregory Peck. The El Rancho fell on hard times after World War II and at one point it was closed down by federal agents who discovered an illegal gambling casino in a back room. In the late 1980s local entrepreneur Armand Ortega restored the hotel to its former glory and the El Rancho is now definitely worth a visit, even if it is only for a stroll through the ornate two-story lobby, decorated with autographed pictures of some of the celebrities who've checked in.

The El Rancho's restaurant is very good, or try either **Earl's**—the favorite of *Crosswinds* food critic Sharon Niederman, who praises the green chile chicken enchiladas—or the **Eagle**—Albuquerque's Rabbi Lynn Gottlieb likes the authentic lamb stew with hominy.

If you're of the shopping persuasion, don't miss Gallup's famous trading posts and pawn shops, used by local Indians for generations as a source of quick cash. The best and most authentic of the lot is **Richardson's Trading Company,** a longtime operation

(1913) with an amazing variety of intriguing merchandise. Another good bet is the Tanner Family's **Shush Yaz Trading Company,** which has a café that serves Native American food. Here, as at other pawn shops in Navajoland, the best values are often "old" or "dead" pawn: collectible items that were exchanged for loans so long ago that their original owners can't be found or are no longer alive.

If You Go: The **El Rancho (863-9311)** is at **1000 East Hwy 66,** **Richardson's** at **222 West Hwy 66, Shush Yaz** at **214 West Aztec,** **Earl's** at **1400 East Hwy 66,** and the **Eagle** at **West Hwy 66 at the Railroad Yards.** For information contact the **Gallup Convention and Visitors Bureau: 800-242-4282.** And, yes, Indians do form a majority of the population here. Turn on the radio and you'll hear country tunes by Reba McIntyre or Garth Brooks introduced in Navajo.

10 *Best* Native American Celebration

Western humorist Will Rogers went so far as to label it "the greatest American show." Each year since 1922 the **Inter-Tribal Indian Ceremonial** has been held at **Red Rock Museum and State Park,** east of Gallup, and it's now one of the country's largest celebrations of its indigenous culture. Besides ceremonial dances and other traditional powwow events (all of which you're welcome to photograph), visitors can browse among stalls selling more than $10-million worth of jewelry, rugs, ceramics, and wood carvings. There's traditional food on sale, too.

Red Rock is set beneath awe-inspiring red sandstone cliffs that seem to encircle the area. Besides the spectacular setting— which offers camping, horseback riding, and picnicking facilities—there's a convention center and indoor auditorium. Each evening during summer, traditional Indian dances are performed for tourists (admission is $3) in the outdoor amphitheater. The place comes alive on many weekends for rodeos, a hot air balloon fiesta, powwows, concerts, and demolition derbies.

"The tall, red cliffs are amazing," says M. L. Duncan, a landscape architect who visits here with his wife, librarian Valerie

Brooker. "They're definitely the best-looking sandstone formations I've ever seen in New Mexico—and I've seen hundreds."

If You Go: The **Inter-Tribal** is held for one week beginning the second Thursday of August at **Red Rock Museum and State Park (863-3896 or 722-3839),** 5 miles east of Gallup on NM 566; take the Red Rock exit off I-40. Many Inter-Tribal participants stay overnight in the state park during this event, so you're best off finding accommodations elsewhere.

Insider Tip Near Red Rock is the historic **Outlaw Trading Post,** built beneath the formation in 1888, and a small museum that also maintains a desert botanical garden. Open daily, 8:00 A.M. to 9:00 P.M. Museum admission is $1 for adults, 50¢ for children.

11 *Best* Mining Museum

An exact replica of a uranium mine fills the deep basement of the fascinating **Museum of Mining** in Grants—which once billed itself as "the atomic city" in recognition of its proximity to the world's largest uranium mines. The industry flourished from the early 1950s until the market crashed after the 1979 Three Mile Island nuclear disaster, eventually putting 8,000 men and women out of work. Take an elevator into Section 26 for a self-guided tour of authentic-looking work areas, drilling equipment, chutes, ventilation shafts, and even the kind of room where workers hung out during blasting operations. Uranium miners who've visited say the place feels like the real thing—and some former miners are occasional tour guides.

"Visiting the museum mine is one of the best ways to understand what this kind of work was all about," says Peter Eichstaedt, the author of a book about the health-related impact of local mining entitled *If You Poison Us: Uranium and Native Americans.* "From the 1950s through the 1970s there was a gold-rush mentality in this part of the country. Unfortunately, a lot of Indians became sick and died because safety concerns were often sacrificed in the name of national defense."

The trip offers a worthwhile glimpse into the gritty (and dangerous) mining way of life, although claustrophobes may want to stay topside and browse among the fine first-floor exhibits, which detail local history.

If You Go: The **Mining Museum (800-748-2142)** is at **100 Iron Street,** at the corner of Santa Fe Avenue. Open daily (except Sunday) during summer from 9:00 A.M. to 7:00 P.M., 9:00 A.M. to 4:00 P.M. the rest of the year. Sunday hours are 1:00 P.M. to 7:00 P.M. Admission is $2; children under eight free.

12 *Best* Photo Opportunity from an Interstate

Laguna Pueblo is made up of six distinct villages, but only one of these catches the casual visitor's eye. And what a catch! Dominating the skyline is the **San José de Laguna Mission Church,** completed in 1705 atop a small hill at the center of this very traditional Indian village. **Old Laguna,** a tight cluster of whitewashed adobes, stretches before westbound freeway travelers in a dramatic vista from I-40. For a closer look at the classic Spanish colonial mission, take Exit 108 and drive or walk through the narrow streets. You can enter the church, but, as is the case at most pueblos, pictures cannot be taken on tribal land without a permit from officials. Inside you'll discover a wonderful carved altar and elaborate religious decoration, all made by skilled Laguna crafts people.

It may sound odd, but Laguna is the "newest" pueblo in New Mexico, founded by immigrants from Cochiti and Santa Domingo pueblos after the region's reconquest by Spain in 1692, 12 years after the Pueblo Revolt successfully expelled the Spanish from New Mexico. For almost two centuries, these Native Americans fought eviction attempts by various government authorities.

"In 1870, the United States decided that the Laguna Indians did have the right to occupy the land given to them by the Spanish crown," notes Jill Schneider, in her book, *Route 66 Across New Mexico.* "I can't help but wonder what the Laguna people thought when the governments of newcomers agreed that the Lagunas should live on [their own] land."

If you like old churches and obscure shrines, check out **Our Lady of Sorrows** in nearby Seboyeta, founded in 1749 as part of the oldest New Mexico Spanish settlement west of the Río Puerco. In a box canyon nearby is an unusual outdoor shrine called **Los Portales,** venerated by local Catholics since the same era.

If You Go: **Laguna Pueblo (552-6001)** is 46 miles west of Albuquerque via I-40. The name *laguna* refers to a small lake that has evaporated over the years and become a meadow where livestock is now grazed. Take the Old Laguna exit if you're heading for Seboyeta, about 9 miles north on NM 279.

> **Insider Tip**
>
> Many Laguna residents support themselves as artists and are best known for their fine pottery, similar in style to that of nearby Ácoma. Good times to buy artwork and visit Laguna are March 19 and September 19, **St. Joseph's Feast Days**, when dancing, eating, and celebrating goes on from sunrise to sundown. Another interesting festival occurs every August on **San Lorenzo's Feast Day,** when everyone named Lorenzo (or Larry, or Lawrence) throws gifts to family and friends from pueblo rooftops.

13 *Best* City on a Mesa Top

Ácoma is known as Sky City for good reason. This most picturesque of Indian pueblos is perched high atop a 376-foot-high mesa that, until relatively recently, could only be scaled via steep foot and burro trails. The dramatic seven-acre site was chosen more than 1,300 years ago for its obvious strategic value. (Ácoma vies with Taos Pueblo and the Hopi tribe's Oraibi for the title of oldest continuously-inhabited community in the United States.)

When they arrived at Ácoma in 1540, even the Spanish conquistadors were impressed, until 13 of their men were killed in a surprise attack. A second, better-equipped force led by Juan de Oñate plotted revenge in 1599: more than 70 Indians were killed in that battle and scores were taken prisoner. Men over the age of 25 had one foot cut off as punishment. Spaniards later sold these and other Ácoma captives, including women and children, into 20 years of slavery in Mexico. No wonder that when the Spanish reconquered New Mexico after the Pueblo Revolt of 1680, the Ácoma were the last tribe to be subdued in 1699.

Life atop the mesa has always been difficult and to this day there is no electricity, school bus service, or running water for the 15-or-so families who still live here year-round. Homes are built of mud and straw hauled up the mesa's steep trails on the backs of men and pack animals. Many Ácoma houses are used as summer or spiritual retreats by tribal members who live elsewhere. Many Ácomites earn a living by selling their fine handmade pottery to tourists. These clay pots are known for their distinctive black-and-white patterns, which depict birds, animals, and human figures.

"Non-Indians are amazed that our people could survive up here," says Jeff Valdo, a native of nearby Ácomita who works as a chef in Santa Fe. "But many of them prefer this quiet and isolated way of life."

A high point of any visit is a quiet moment inside the cool recesses of **San Esteban del Rey de Ácoma,** a simple but exceptionally beautiful Catholic church built by forced Indian labor between 1629 and 1641. San Esteban is one of the finest examples of Spanish colonial architecture in New Mexico, all the more remarkable considering that the materials used in its construction were carried up the sides of the mesa. This includes 40-foot pine beams cut in mountain forests more than 30 miles away and hauled up using yucca ropes. San Esteban was faithfully restored during the 1920s and is the setting for a lovely candlelight mass every Christmas Eve. You'll note that, because it doubled as a fortress, there are no windows in San Esteban and the walls are seven feet thick. The painting of Saint Joseph that hangs inside the church was a gift of Spain's King Philip II and is said to have miraculous powers.

If You Go: Ácoma's Sky City (800-747-0181) is 13 miles south of I-40, reached on Tribal Road 38 via either Exit 96 (west) or 107 (east) on NM 23. The pueblo is about 70 miles west of Albuquerque. There's a per-person fee of up to $5 to visit Sky City (using a sliding scale based on age). Hours are 8:00 A.M. to 6:00 P.M. daily April to October, 8:00 A.M. to 4:30 P.M. the rest of the year (except for religious holidays when Ácoma is closed). A $5 camera fee must be paid by photographers (no camcorders allowed). Non-Ácoma visitors can enter the pueblo only on a one-hour tour, after registering and paying a fee at the tribal museum at the base of the mesa. Escorted transportation by minivan is provided, up a road built in 1957 by a Hollywood movie company. You're allowed to walk down on a steep trail, an experience that's highly recommended. Food and gifts are sold at the visitors' center.

Insider Tip En route to Sky City from the northeast you'll pass **Enchanted Mesa,** a 400-foot promontory said to be the original home of the Ácoma tribe, until a rock slide cut off passage to the village on its flat peak. It is now unoccupied and considered sacred. Exiting I-40 from the northwest, you'll see an exact, small-scale replica of San Esteban that was built earlier this century in the Ácoma village of McCartys.

14 *Best* Lava Flow

Nancy McMillan, a geologist at New Mexico State University, says the early Spanish explorers were the first to call the state's biggest and best lava flow *el malpais,* or, "the bad land." The forbidding name has stuck, although local usage has been corrupted to 'the mal-pie' and much of this desolate area southeast of Grants has been turned into a national monument.

"It looks like what you imagine the surface of the moon to resemble," says McMillan, noting that New Mexico has a long and rich volcanic history. "Two huge mountains northeast of El Malpais—Mount Taylor and Redondo Peak—were once among the tallest and most active volcanoes in what is now the United States.

"This is a wonderful place to hike, particularly during the milder weather of spring and fall," McMillan says, noting that summer temperatures often soar above 100°F among the jagged black rocks, which can rip the soles off tennis shoes. The longest trail here was originally made by the ancient Anasazi and it winds for more than 7 miles across the lava flow. Still intact are bridges made of lava rocks that were piled across fissures by the Indians.

Shorter treks take visitors to tall sandstone bluffs (**Cibola Wilderness Trail,** off NM 117) and the **El Calderón Bat Cave** (rangers lead evening hikes on summer weekends to watch the bats emerge from this cave's narrow lava tubes). **Junction Cave,** a convoluted 17-mile-long lava tube, encompasses two smaller caves (**Big Skylight** and **Four-Window**) and can be reached on foot or by four-wheel-drive vehicle via Cibola County Road 42 (off NM 53). The Anasazi and El Calderón trailheads are on NM 53, farther south.

"The best place to get an overview of El Malpais is from the Sandstone Bluffs overlook [10 miles south of I-40 on NM 117]," says McMillan, who confesses to a special fascination with the oddball pockets of fertile soil, ice, and water that get trapped in the impenetrable lava formations.

If You Go: Access to **El Malpais** is via I-40 to either NM 117 or NM 53 (between Grants and McCartys), then south about 10 miles. The park can be reached from the south via Zuni or Quemado on the same state highways. (El Malpais actually lies between the two as they run parallel in a north-south direction.) You can picnic and camp among the 262,000 acres of ravaged lava flows, cinder cones, ice caves, and other volcanic residue, although facilities are limited. Besides rustic camping at the monument, accommodations are available at Grants, Ramah, and El Morro. Also recommended is the **Vogt Ranch (783-4362),** a two-room B&B in a comfortable and historic ranchhouse off NM 53 a few miles east of Ramah. Maps, brochures, and program schedules are available at **park headquarters (285-5406),** open 8:00 A.M. to 4:30 P.M. daily and located on NM 117 about 7 miles south of I-40.

Insider Tip A private holding within El Malpais is the **Bandera Crater and Ice Cave (783-4303),** about 20 miles south of Grants off NM 53. The price of admission is steep ($5) for these mild curiosities: an 800-foot volcanic cone (one of five in the area) and a lava tube that contains glacier-like ice deposits up to 20 feet thick and hundreds of years old. The gray-green ice,

sheltered and insulated by thick lava, is formed by conden-
sation and windswept snow. Decidedly commercial, this
destination will be of most interest to die-hard volcano
buffs and those who appreciate old-time trading posts.
More worthy of your time is **La Ventana,** a natural sandstone arch (New Mexico's largest) located about 200 yards
off NM 117 (watch for signs) and about 17 miles south of I-40.

15 Best Ancient Graffiti

The inscription of Juan de Oñate at Inscription Rock, El Morro
National Monument.

Inscription Rock, at **El Morro
National Monument,** is a
kind of sandstone blackboard,
upon which travelers have for
centuries left their mark. The
roster of names on this sheer,
200-foot rock includes Juan de
Oñate, one of New Mexico's
first Spanish explorers, who
guided New Mexico's first
European colonists north
from Mexico in 1598. He cut
his name into the exposed
rock, already adorned with
Indian artistry hundreds of years old, on his return trip in 1605.
Scores of other names, declarations, and even poetry were added
to Inscription Rock over the next 300 years, until the National
Park Service made this the country's first national monument in
1906. (If you feel overwhelmed by the desire to write your name
on a rock, a slab of sandstone has been installed next to the visitors' center for that purpose.)

Travelers have camped here over the years because a large,
permanent pool of water lies at the base of the rock, formed by an
underground spring and the hundreds of thousands of gallons of
runoff from rain, ice, and snow. (Although it looks tempting, bathing and swimming are prohibited.)

"This has always been a shady and quiet place to refuel and
rest one's weary bones," says Edmund Ladd, a Zuni scholar who

is curator of ethnology for the state's Laboratory of Anthropology. "And strategically speaking, the tall bluff made an excellent lookout."

If you have an extra hour, be sure to climb the stairway to the top of Inscription Rock for a self-guided tour of the abandoned 13th-century Zuni village, **Atsinna,** hidden on the roof of the mesa. You'll note that the construction is almost identical to what you'll see in daily use at Ácoma and Zuni. There's even a secluded box canyon behind Atsinna, full of tall pines and junipers. From the top of the rock, visitors are blessed with a commanding view of the broad valley that constitutes the Zuni homeland,

An example of ancient rock art to be found at El Morro National Monument.

from the green Zuni Mountains rising in the east to the Arizona desert flattening across the mesa-punctured horizon in the west.

If You Go: **El Morro National Monument (783-4226)** is open from 8:00 A.M. to 5:00 P.M. daily (until 8:00 P.M. in summer) for a $3 per-car admission. The village of El Morro, immediately east of the park on NM 53, has a small grocery, restaurant, RV parking and campsites. The monument is 43 miles southwest of Grants. There's a self-guided trail, campground, and picnic area. The visitors' center has restrooms, soda machines, and a good museum.

16 *Best* Mural

Within **Zuni Pueblo's "Old Mission" Catholic Church** resides one of New Mexico's finest modern treasures. Local artist Alex Seowtewa has spent thousands of hours over the past several years restoring the 18th-century interior murals of this mission church to their original brilliance. The murals show birdlike Zuni religious figures representing the four seasons, as well as portraits of the primary Catholic saints. Seowtewa's vivid painting has attracted such admirers as Jacqueline Onassis and Mother Teresa.

La Nuestra Señora de Guadalupe de Zuñi was built in 1699 and restored during the 1960s. (The original chapel was constructed in 1630, but destroyed during the Pueblo Revolt of 1680.) One of Zuni's most talented visual artists, Seowtewa is wholeheartedly devoted to the preservation and celebration of his tribe's heritage—and it shows. In recent years he's been assisted by his son, Kenneth.

"We are a religious people," explained then-pueblo governor Robert Lewis, in a 1989 interview with writer Douglas Preston. "You have to have a belief in something, and faith, and above all be thankful. Enjoy the blessings in a *good* way, and be kind to your neighbors."

The pueblo of Zuni (pronounced ZOO-nee) is perhaps the most culturally unique of all New Mexican tribes. Despite its isolation, the Zunis were the first tribe in the region to have contact with Spanish explorers, who first stumbled through the area in 1527. More Spaniards arrived in 1540 as part of a zealous, greedy quest for the fabled Seven Cities of Cibola, where the streets were supposedly paved with gold.

Through the centuries, Zuni people have fought hard to maintain their sovereignty and in 1970 theirs became the first native community in the United States to fully govern itself. Since then, Zuni has turned its art industry into a major moneymaker, funneling the profits into tribal schools and community improvement projects.

Visitors can find a wide and intriguing selection of fetish carvings. These are stone (sometimes shell) representations of animals such as bears, mountain lions, and coyotes that are used traditionally to bring the bearer strength or good luck in hunting or planting. Some of these small talismans are also used in religious ceremonies. Each carved stone creature carries a bundle, tied with sinew, that often includes an arrowhead, feather, and a shard of turquoise, serpentine, or coral. Once the fetishes are blessed by the Zuni they are said to contain the spirit of the beast they represent.

"The fetish helps capture the spirit of a particular animal in your mind and gives you a new way of looking at things," writes Hal Zina Bennett, who has studied Zuni fetishes and authored a book about them. "In such a highly technological world, we hunger for the other side of [ourselves], the intuitive side, the source of our creativity."

If You Go: Tours of the church, still in use, are free. **Zuni** is 22 miles west of Ramah and 35 miles south of Gallup on NM 53. If you'd like to see the ruins of three ancient pueblos, check with the **tribal offices (782-4481)** in the village. You'll be issued a permit and directions. A number of shops in Zuni sell local arts and crafts. Besides fetishes, the Zuni are known for silver, coral, and turquoise inlay as well as needlepoint jewelry (also called petit point). You can buy this kind of art at the **Zuni Craftsmen Cooperative, Shiwi Trading Post,** and **Turquoise Village,** all on NM 53.

Chapter 7

Northeastern
New Mexico

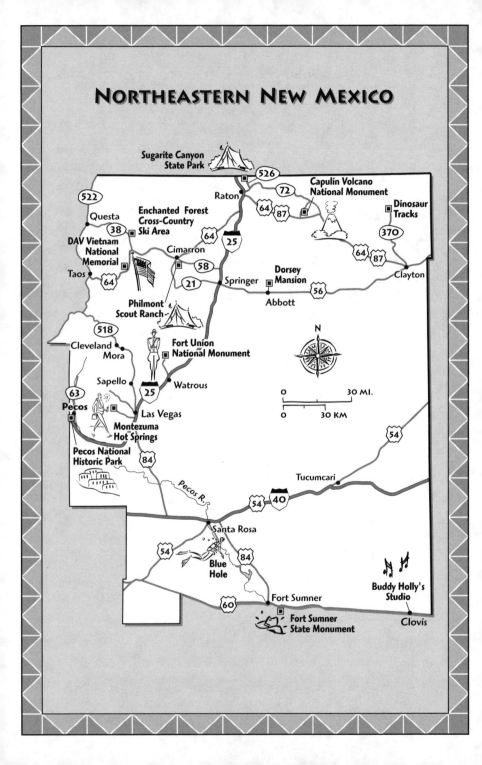

NORTHEASTERN NEW MEXICO

Sugarite Canyon
State Park

526

Capulin Volcano
National Monument

72

Raton

522

Questa

38

Enchanted Forest
Cross-Country
Ski Area

64

87

Dinosaur
Tracks

370

DAV Vietnam
National
Memorial

64

Cimarron

58

64

25

64

87

Taos

64

21

Springer

Dorsey
Mansion

Clayton

56

Philmont
Scout Ranch

Abbott

518

Fort Union
National Monument

N

Cleveland

Mora

Sapello

63

25

Watrous

30 MI.

Pecos

Las Vegas

0   30 KM

Montezuma
Hot Springs

54

Pecos National
Historic Park

84

Pecos R.

Tucumcari

54

40

Santa Rosa

54

84

Blue
Hole

Buddy Holly's
Studio

60

Fort Sumner

Clovis

Fort Sumner
State Monument

What's Best about Northeastern New Mexico

This is where the Great Plains meet the Rockies, the cowboy meets the shepherd, the miner meets the mountain man. The northeast quadrant of New Mexico encompasses a dramatic landscape that is by turns vast and arid, green and mountainous. It is one of the few areas of the state where indigenous people—Plains Indians—left few artifacts, where Spanish colonists founded almost no settlements, and where Wild West stereotypes are still apparent in architecture, history, and attitudes. This is largely due to the area's physical isolation, extremes of climate, limited resources, and the dominance of aggressive tribes until the mid-nineteenth century.

The most northeasterly portion of this region doesn't look any different than the short-grass prairies of Colorado, Kansas, Texas, and Oklahoma that stretch for endless miles across the border. The terrain changes dramatically toward the center of New Mexico, however, where the last lofty peaks of the Rocky Mountains thrust their way south, creating a wide range of climatic and vegetative zones dominated by piñon-juniper woodlands, pine savannas, aspen canyons, mixed-conifer forests, and alpine tundra.

This part of the state has more of a frontier feel than any other. The native people of this area were mostly nomadic, and the Spanish and Mexican presence was barely felt here. Not until the United States took over the territory in 1846 did permanent settlement begin on a wide scale. After a railroad-induced boom that began in 1880, the northeast settled into an economy largely based on agriculture, including timber, cattle ranching, and farming.

For our purposes, this quadrant of New Mexico is defined as including the eastern slopes of the Rocky Mountains, the plains north of I-40, and the communities of Las Vegas, Mora, Ratón, Cimarron, Santa Rosa, Clayton, Roy, Springer, and Clovis.

1 Best Place to Make Wine

As one drives east of Santa Fe on I-25, the wide road winds through the lush, emerald foothills of the Sangre de Cristo Mountains. This is an ancient trade and travel route, used for centuries by Plains and Pueblo Indians.

Today you can see evidence of that commerce at **Pecos National Historic Park,** between the villages of Pecos and Rowe, where the remains of the long-abandoned Cicuye Indian village is preserved (and worth a visit). Not far away, tiny Spanish-speaking hamlets along the side roads testify to the later occupation by settlers from Spain and Mexico.

Turn off I-25 at the Villanueva exit and head south on NM 3 (Exit 323) for a closer look at these unpretentious communities in one of the Pecos River's loveliest valleys. The villages seem stuck in time—their plastered adobe homes have changed little during the past century.

At El Barranca, you'll come upon the **Madison Winery,** which produces some of the best wines in the state from some of New Mexico's oldest vines. Visitors are welcome to taste Madison's several varieties of award-winning wines, including many made from French hybrid grapes. Tasting is done in the rambling, tree-shaded adobe of the owners, Bill and Elise Madison. A friendly couple, the Madisons have revived high-quality wine making in the Villanueva Valley against great odds.

"Madison is my favorite winery," says Charlotte Plantz, a ceramic artist and volunteer grape picker who lives in nearby San José. "I love the people and I love the wine."

Stock up at the winery for an afternoon in the country. There are campsites, hiking trails, fishing holes, and picnic grounds nearby along the Pecos River near Villanueva, Anton Chico, Terrero, and Cowles.

"Villanueva is the best small Hispanic village within an hour's drive of Santa Fe," says Albuquerque photographer Merilyn Brown, whose post-card images are sold throughout the state. "It's in a beautiful location on a hilltop overlooking the Pecos. There are lots of old adobes with pitched tin roofs."

Be sure to stop at the **Catholic church** to see an amazing folk art needlepoint tapestry—265 feet long—made by 36 local women in 1976 to commemorate the U.S. Bicentennial with a colorful representation of local history. The church is made of local stone with an exterior worship grotto. If the front door's locked, try the side entrance.

If You Go: Madison Winery (800-708-9463) is open from 10:00 A.M. to 6:00 P.M., Monday through Saturday, noon to 6:00 P.M. Sundays. Take the Villanueva exit from I-25 and head south about 4 miles to the winery. The village of Villanueva and its adjacent state park are about 3 miles farther south.

Insider Tip Madison's success is due in part to the help of family members, neighbors, and customers who volunteer during harvest time (September–October) to pick and crush grapes. These are wonderful daylong events, culminating in a potluck feast and sampling of the product. The picking can't begin until the grapes' sugar content is exactly right, so call ahead to find out when volunteers are needed.

2 *Best* Victorian Architecture

Welcome to the *other* Las Vegas—the one with a longer history and more character, less glitz and glamour, than the one in Nevada. Founded in 1835 under authority of the then-prevailing Mexican government, *this* Las Vegas quickly became the biggest city in New Mexico. Later, after the United States took control of the territory from Mexico, Las Vegas became a busy mercantile hub for Santa Fe Trail wagon trains and an important rail stop for east-west trains. With prosperity came construction of many houses and commercial buildings. Today more than 900 of these structures are on the National Register of Historic Places: that's nearly half the total number in New Mexico! If you like nineteenth-century Victorian, Queen Anne, Romanesque, Italianate, and Eastlake architectural designs, Las Vegas is the town for you. (A slow economic decline that began in 1905 has discouraged developers from demolishing these buildings.)

"So commonplace and authentic is the territorial-era architecture that dozens of moviemakers have come here to capture the look on film," notes songwriter and humorist Jim Terr, a Las Vegas native whose music can be heard in Roger Vadim's *And God Created Woman*, filmed in the area in 1987. "I grew up in an old brick house built in 1910—the town's full of 'em."

A good base for exploration is the three-story **Plaza Hotel,** built in an Italianate bracketed style on the town plaza in 1882. Fully restored with many antiques, the elegant structure houses a B&B and a full-service restaurant. Even if you don't plan to check in or eat a meal (food and service is unexceptional), a stroll through the well-appointed bar **(Byron T's)**, lobby, and conservatory is highly recommended. There's even a resident ghost.

Detailed walking-tour maps of the downtown area are available in the Plaza Hotel lobby and at many other Las Vegas businesses. It's fun to spend an hour or two admiring the wonderful old buildings along the streets that radiate from the old plaza, particularly Fifth, Sixth, Seventh, Washington, and Columbia. Among the best preserved buildings are the **Carnegie Library, Hotel Casteneda, Ifield Law Office, Immaculate Conception School, Our Lady of Sorrows Catholic Church,** and the **D. T. Lowery House.** There are antique stores full of amazing things and several worthwhile art galleries. Many artists also open their studios to visitors.

A historical curiosity is the **Rough Riders Museum.** It commemorates the feisty soldiers organized by Teddy Roosevelt for his famous Cuban campaign during the Spanish-American War. Because many of the volunteers came from New Mexico, a Rough Rider reunion was held at the Hotel Casteneda in Las Vegas every year from 1899 to 1967. Besides historical objects and memorabilia, the museum contains many items relating to the region's history.

In early June the chamber of commerce sponsors a **Rails 'n' Trails celebration,** commemorating the important roles played hereabouts by both the Santa Fe Trail and the ATSF Railroad. The three-day event includes a parade, rodeo, cook-off, Tom Mix film festival (Mix made dozens of movies here), quilt show, horse-drawn trolley tours, music, dancing, and a model railroad extravaganza.

If You Go: Contact the **Las Vegas Chamber of Commerce** at **800-832-5947**. The **Plaza Hotel (425-3591)** is at **230 Old Town Plaza**. The **Spic & Span (425-6481)**, at **713 Douglas Street**, is open for breakfast and lunch, serving New Mexican dishes as well as excellent baked goods. Locals in the know say the best green chile is served at **El Rialto Café (454-0037), 141 Bridge Street**. The **Rough Riders Museum (425-8726)** is at **727 Grand Avenue**. It's open from 9:00 A.M. to 4:00 P.M., Monday through Saturday. There's no admission charge and Curator Harold Thatcher is a wealth of information. If you're inclined to spend the night in a genuine Las Vegas mansion, try the **Carriage House B&B (454-1784)**, a three-story, five-bedroom Queen Anne built in 1893. It's elegantly appointed and nicely restored, at **925 Sixth Street**. The name Las Vegas, by the way, is Spanish for "the meadows," a reference to the short-grass prairie that spreads along the banks of the Gallinas River.

3 *Best* Outdoor Hot Springs

Montezuma Hot Springs was once a popular turn-of-the-century spa catering to railroad passengers shuttled from nearby Las Vegas to the 1884 **Montezuma Hotel,** an impressive three-story, red sandstone Victorian structure now owned by United World College, which has its small campus near the bubbling, therapeutic thermal waters across the Gallinas River. (Though imposing, the "castle" needs millions of dollars worth of repairs and is not open to visitors.)

The Montezuma bathhouse was closed many years ago and the adjacent springs are now open to the sky and free of charge. The college owns the cement-enclosed springs and bathers use them at their own risk. The springs are kept clean by volunteers and the setting is pleasant: a narrow, wooded canyon. The natural hot tubs are rather exposed, however, and nude bathing is not allowed.

"This is a great place for travelers to soak away their cares and woes, as others have done before them for generations," says Phil Archuleta, a Pecos Wilderness guide who was raised near here.

If You Go: The **Montezuma Hot Springs** are located 9 miles northwest of Las Vegas and a few steps from NM 65 on the campus of the Armand Hammer World College. Look for a "HOT SPRINGS" sign on the highway's shoulder.

Insider Tip About 0.5 mile farther down the road is a pond that freezes solid in winter, providing one of the only easily accessible outdoor ice-skating rinks in New Mexico. Like the hot springs, it's free: first come, first served. Continue down windy, narrow NM 65 into Gallinas Canyon and you'll see some of the prettiest mountain scenery in New Mexico. There are several national forest picnic sites and campgrounds here, as well as trailheads for Elk Mountain and Hermit's Peak. If you like nature, you'll love this backcountry. If you want to stay, check out **Mountain Music Guest Ranch (425-7008)**, which offers cabins, horseback riding, and fishing.

4 Best Stargazing

The **Star Hill Inn** is a mountain lodge with a difference. This amateur astronomers' retreat is designed as a getaway for people who like to look at the stars. With this in mind, its owners have chosen a tranquil, scenic spot in the Rockies where the mountain air is clear and clean, with almost no "light pollution" from neighboring cities. Located at an altitude of 7,200 feet, the 195-acre grounds are covered with vanilla-scented ponderosa pines and constitute a haven for coyotes, deer, and the occasional bear or elk.

According to *The Sidereal Times*, a publication of the Albuquerque Astronomical Society, Star Hill "offers to amateur astronomers and their families one of the most beautiful and comfortable settings for stargazing in North America." Similar sentiments have been expressed by visitors from all over the world.

"We love getting away from the phones for a weekend in a Star Hill cabin," says jazz flutist Herbie Mann, a Santa Fe resident who escapes here with his wife, writer Janeal Arison. "It's out in the middle of nowhere and the night sky is wonderful. During the day it is the kind of quintessential blue that touches my heart and spirit in a way I've never before experienced."

Phil Mahon, the former Dallas minister who developed Star Hill with his artist wife, Blair, knows of only three other astronomy-themed lodges in the world: one each in Hawaii, France, and Arizona.

Besides a fireplace and private porch, each of the seven cozy cabins has a fully equipped kitchen, shades for daytime sleeping, and, of course, ready access to a (rented) telescope of up to 22 inches in diameter in a communal viewing area, away from cottage lights. You can also bring your own telescope, or sign up for a guided tour of the heavens using Star Hill's Compustar 14-inch Celestron. On a typical night, you'll get a close-up view of planets, star clusters, nebulae, and the moon. A warm library with star charts and astronomy videos (as well as cookies) is a few steps away.

The area also affords opportunities for hiking, fishing, golfing, cross-country skiing, and birding. There are volleyball, badminton, and barbecue facilities on the premises. Instruction in astronomy and birding is provided during periodic seminars.

If You Go: Star Hill Inn (425-5605) is 10 miles north of Las Vegas, a few miles west of NM 518 near the village of Sapello. Reservations are required due to limited space and a two-night minimum is preferred. Food isn't provided at Star Hill, but recommended dining options include previously mentioned Las Vegas restaurants and the **Pendaries Village Country Club** (425-6076), 28 miles north of Las Vegas on NM 105 and open May to mid-October.

5 *Best* Raspberries

Mora, one of New Mexico's smallest and most isolated counties, is prime berry-growing territory, hence its name ("blackberry" in Spanish). And although wild berries are found here in abundance, the real prize is Mora's commercial raspberry crop. Thousands of these delectable morsels are harvested in late summer at the **Salman family ranch,** which includes the town site of **La Cueva,** now a National Historic Site.

"Besides delicious raspberries, you can buy farm-grown fruit, dried flowers, herbs, and nursery stock at the ranch," notes Debora Bluestone, a computer instructor and longtime Las Vegas resident. "I always call to check the availability of raspberries, which usually reach their peak ripeness in September." She also checks out the packaged goods sold at **Salman's La Cueva store,** including prize-winning raspberry jam, syrup, and vinegar,

An added attraction is the historic water-driven **La Cueva Mill,** built on the property in the 1870s to provide wheat flour to Fort Union soldiers and Santa Fe Trail immigrants. It was used to grind wheat and generate electricity until 1949. The old wheel still turns and the venerable grindstone is on display nearby.

Across the street is a small ranch-owned café that sells homemade sandwiches, Frito pies, tamales, nachos, and fresh bread. Ever try a hot dog with raspberry mustard? Highly recommended is a delicious raspberry-lemon slush called "razzleade" and soft-serve ice cream topped with raspberry syrup. Next door is the **San Rafael Mission,** a nineteenth-century adobe church with distinctive Gothic windows installed by French missionary priests.

If You Go: **Salman Ranch (387-2900)** is 6 miles south of Mora at the junction of NM 518 and NM 442. During the growing and harvest season, it's open from 9:00 A.M. to 5:00 P.M., Tuesday through Sunday; shorter hours November through April. Fresh raspberries are usually available from early August through September.

6 *Best* Roller Mill

What the heck is a roller mill, you ask. It's a water-powered flour mill that uses cast-iron rollers to grind wheat, corn, and other grains. Visit the **Cleveland Roller Mill Historical Museum** for a fascinating closer look. Built during the 1890s, this adobe structure was used until 1954 and has been fully restored by a local group that maintains it as a "living history" museum. The mill—one of the few of its kind remaining in the United States—is still owned by the Cassidy family, which acquired it in 1913 from the German who built it.

"The fact that the Cleveland Mill was functioning into the atomic age is testimony to the enduring rural lifestyle and poverty of Mora County," says local historian Alex Downey. "A visit to the mill provides an interesting peek at the area's not-so-distant past and is an important portion of New Mexico's history."

The Cleveland Roller Mill.

Be sure to see the informative 12-minute video that explains the mill's operation and Mora County's historic 1850–1940 role as New Mexico's breadbasket. There are fascinating old-time photos on display, as well as contemporary exhibits. With the decline of wheat farming, Mora County's population dropped from about 13,000 in 1910 to less than 6,500 in 1996.

If You Go: The **Cleveland Roller Mill (387-2645)** is about 32 miles north of Las Vegas on NM 518. Admission is $3 for adults; open 10:00 A.M. to 5:00 P.M. daily from Memorial Day through October 31. There's a pleasant picnic area and an 1890s New Mexico stone gristmill next to the museum. Several motels and home-style restaurants are 2 miles east in Mora, where the **St. Vrain Mill** (circa 1850) can be seen. Campgrounds are nearby at Morphy Lake and Coyote Creek state parks.

Insider Tip If you're here for the **Cleveland Millfest** on Labor Day weekend, you can see the mill's massive, intricate machinery actually produce and sack flour, an amazing feat considering the age of the belts, chains, and other mechanical parts. Another good time to come is during the annual August arts and crafts festival.

7 *Best* Cross-Country Skiing

The **Enchanted Forest Cross-Country Ski Area** is a privately operated network of Nordic ski trails located near 9,850-foot Bobcat Pass, northeast of Taos.

"My boyfriend Guy and I have skied all over New Mexico, and we like Enchanted Forest the best," declares Linda Pearson, a cross-country fan since childhood. "It's never crowded and the facilities are terrific."

Enchanted Forest maintains more than 18 miles of groomed trails that meander through 600 acres of meadows and forests in the Carson National Forest. Skill levels ranges from easy to difficult, with signs clearly posting each route. You can rent ski equipment and arrange for instruction at the Enchanted Forest office in town.

For downhill skiers there are two nearby choices: **Red River Ski Area (754-2382)** a few miles west of Enchanted Forest on NM 38 and **Ski Rio (586-1240)**, 44 miles north near Costilla on NM 196. **Red River's Chamber of Commerce** answers questions at **754-2366.**

Not to be missed is the **Just Desserts Eat and Ski event,** held in late February, when skiers are served scrumptious deserts (i.e., hot fudge sundaes) at each of a dozen or more "stations" along the trails. Burning calories was never more fun (or tasty).

If You Go: Enchanted Forest (754-2374) is 3 miles east of Red River on NM 38; open daily during ski season. There are many restaurant, hotel, and condo options in Red River, an old mining town that's been revived by winter sports enthusiasts.

8 *Best* Military Memorial

The **DAV (Disabled American Veterans) Vietnam Veterans National Memorial** is one of New Mexico's most unusual—and poignant—landmarks. Its heart is a privately built, nondenominational chapel enshrined to the memory of the thousands of men and women who were killed or disabled in the Vietnam War. The dove-shaped structure rises to about 50 feet and sits next to an equally contemporary-looking visitors' center.

"If we have to have war memorials," said one visitor, who preferred to remain anonymous, "this is the way they should be made. The DAV is simple, yet powerful."

Built between 1968 and 1971 by grieving Dr. Victor Westphall, whose son David was killed in Vietnam, this monument predates the better known Vietnam Memorial in Washington, D.C., which was dedicated about a decade later. As in the nation's capital, thousands of vets converge here each Memorial Day to honor their fallen comrades.

"I created the memorial and have spent much of the past 25 years there," says Westphall, "and yet it still fills me with awe. This place is far more powerful than I expected it to be—and that's the case for most visitors I've talked with."

The Disabled American Veterans organization helped Westphall add the visitors' center, where a video and still photos explain why and how the shrine came about. No government funds have been involved. Westphall lives part-time in an apartment on the premises and is happy to answer questions. No matter how you feel about the Vietnam War, you won't come away from this place unmoved.

If You Go: The **DAV Vietnam Veterans National Memorial (377-6900)** perches on a hill between Angel Fire and Eagle Nest on NM 64. There is no admission charge. The visitors' center is open daily from 6:30 A.M. to 5:30 P.M.; the chapel never closes. The drive to the memorial takes travelers through some beautiful country: grassy, wide valleys surrounded by tall mountain peaks. Every so often there's a small community where basic services are available. Be careful during the long winter, when heavy, sudden snowfalls are not unusual.

_9_ *Best* Place to See the Old Santa Fe Trail

Deep wagon ruts along the famous immigrant trail that brought thousands of pioneers west can still be seen near **Fort Union National Monument,** north of I-25 near Watrous, as well as at other places alongside the freeway. Some of these indentations were made more than 170 years ago, although most travel along the 850-mile trail occurred between 1846 and 1879.

Long-abandoned Fort Union was one of three military posts that have occupied this remote site since 1851, defending the area against everything from Indian raids to an attempted (and unsuccessful) Confederate takeover of New Mexico. There was also a small hospital here that tended to sick or injured travelers and army men. Soldiers stationed here served as armed escorts, riding out to meet wagon trains and mail stages heading toward the Santa Fe Plaza from Old Franklin, Missouri. This spot, near a year-round spring, was chosen because two forks of the trail came together a few miles to the south. The fort closed in 1891 after railroad travel made the route obsolete. Its buildings quickly fell into ruin and are slowly disappearing into the earth.

There's a museum and visitors' center, and self-guided tours are encouraged. An outdoor sound system has been installed that allows you to hear bugle calls and military commands as you walk along the trail. The best time to visit is an hour after dawn or before nightfall, when the low rays of the sun illuminate the wagon ruts and ruins in dramatic relief. The ruts are otherwise sometimes hard to make out due to wind and water erosion over the intervening years.

"Many ladies dislike Fort Union," one military wife observed a century ago. "It has always been noted for severe dust storms. Situated on a barren plain ... it has the most exposed position of any military fort in New Mexico."

If You Go: To reach **Fort Union (425-8025)** take I-25 east of Las Vegas for 26 miles to Exit 336, then proceed 8 miles north on NM 161. Open daily from 8:00 A.M. to 5:00 P.M. (6:00 P.M. in summer) with a $3-per-car admission. There are restrooms and picnic tables, but no camping. On the way to the monument you may see elk or antelope, both plentiful in this grassy area, and ruts of the original Mountain Branch of the Santa Fe Trail. Ask for the "Sites and Structures" handout at the monument to use as a guide to visible relics along the road back to I-25. Head north and you'll see ruts of the old trail for some distance along the west side of I-25.

Insider Tip During summer weekends, park service employees sometimes dress in period costumes, move into drafty tents, and reenact the lives of typical immigrant families who traveled the Santa Fe Trail, answering questions about this important period of American history.

10 *Best* Mansion in the Middle of Nowhere

The **Dorsey Mansion** was once the headquarters of a 60-mile-wide ranch. This was more than a century ago and the spread has been cut down a wee bit, but the ranch house is still impressive. Built out of oiled logs and red sandstone in 1878 by Stephen Dorsey, the 36-room home once boasted three swimming pools and a rose garden that spelled out the name of Dorsey's beloved wife, Helen, in shrubbery.

"All this was created in one of the most remote places in New Mexico," notes Riki Stevens, who grew up on a nearby cattle ranch. "And it's *still* just as remote."

Gothic stone gargoyles—bearing the faces of Mr. and Mrs. Dorsey, naturally—still stare from the rooftop while carved wild-cats and rattlesnakes lunge from an elaborate fountain. Inside is an Italian marble fireplace, crystal chandelier, and swooping stairway banister.

"The Dorsey was remodeled and relandscaped in the early 1990s," says horse trainer Mark Truelove, who lives and works in the area. "The mansion is now definitely worth the drive."

A registered historic landmark, the mansion has at various times been a tuberculosis sanitarium, post office, B&B, and private residence since the Dorseys left (under troubled financial circumstances) in 1892. It is currently a working ranch, raising llamas and horses, and owned by a California physician. Meals and overnight accommodations are *not* provided.

If You Go: From Springer take US 56 about 24 miles east (immediately past Abbott) and head north, following the signs 12 miles on a dead-end dirt road. Although a caretaker is at the mansion most days, it's a good idea to call ahead **(375-2222)** or else the gates may be locked. Admission is $5 per adult and the tour takes about half an hour.

11 Best Historical Museum and Victorian Hotel

Cimarron is one of several historic "gateway" communities that have long straddled the unique transition zone between the vast Great Plains and the rugged mountains of the West. Stretching in one direction from the town is lonesome prairie and in the other is scenic Cimarron Canyon, winding into the verdant forests of the Rockies.

"The **Old Aztec Mill** is our favorite museum," declare David and Betsy Tighe, who renovate old New Mexico houses and write about gourmet cooking, respectively. "The nearby **St. James Hotel** is our favorite romantic getaway."

The mill was converted to its present function in 1967. Built in 1864 by legendary rancher Lucien Bonaparte Maxwell, the Aztec mill produced thousands of barrels of flour from grain grown on some of the 1.7 million acres owned by Maxwell. (This single gristmill is all that's left of what was once the largest private real estate empire in the Western Hemisphere.)

The mill's three-story rock walls are impressive and within them are housed fascinating exhibits documenting pioneer life in nineteenth-century New Mexico. An ideal headquarters for exploring this neck of the woods is the St. James Hotel. Built in 1873 by a former cook for Abraham Lincoln and Ulysses Grant, this thick-walled pink adobe was long considered one of the finest hostelries in the West. Reopened in 1985, visitors can sleep in accommodations once frequented by Jesse James, Annie Oakley, Buffalo Bill Cody, and Wyatt Earp.

It's said that a total of 26 people were shot to death inside the St. James during its rowdier days: you can still see bullet holes in the pressed-tin ceiling. Thankfully, there were peaceful days, too: Zane Grey wrote a novel here and Frederic Remington painted pictures of Western life.

The current owners have gone to great lengths to furnish the guest rooms with authentic Victorian-era antiques and artwork. The hotel restaurant, **Lambert's** (named after founder Henry Lambert), is a treasure. It serves continental meals in a romantic, turn-of-the-century setting. Ask about the 100-year-old resident ghost.

The St. James Hotel.

If You Go: Guided tours of the **St. James Hotel (376-2664)** are $3. The hotel is on NM 21 (Collison Road) near its intersection with US 64. The **Old Aztec Mill Museum (376-2913)** is a block south of the hotel and open weekdays (except Thursday) from 9:00 A.M. to 5:00 P.M., from 1:00 to 5:00 P.M. on weekends. Admission is $2 for adults and $1 for seniors, children under 12, or Scouts in uniform. Cimarron is 19 miles west of I-25 via NM 58. The turnoff is 5 miles north of Springer (at Exit 419).

12 *Best* Boy Scout Ranch

A worthy attraction near Cimarron is the **Philmount Scout Ranch,** a 215-square-mile gift to the Boy Scouts of America from Oklahoma oil man Waite Phillips (of Phillips Petroleum fame). Since 1939, thousands of youngsters from all over the world have spent part of their summers here learning how to live in the great out-doors.

Part of the place is still a working ranch, with cattle, horses, burros, and bison. The **Philmount Museum** and **Seton Library** tell all about it. During the summer, daily tours are given of nearby **Villa Philmonte,** the lavish Spanish Mediterranean-style mansion built by Phillips as his family's retreat.

Heading south on NM 21, about 12 miles from Cimarron, the traveler passes through **Rayado,** the first European settlement in northeastern New Mexico. Kit Carson lived here for about 16 months, trying (unsuccessfully) to farm and raise mules for use on the Santa Fe Trail, which ran past his front door. Carson's at-tractive adobe has been rebuilt and is now a small museum that's operated by the Boy Scouts and open June through August from 9 A.M. to 4 P.M. Old-time activities such as candle making and bread making are demonstrated by scouts.

If You Go: The **Philmount Scout Ranch (376-2281)** is 4 miles south of Cimarron on NM 21. The facility is open to visitors daily from 8:00 A.M. to noon and 1:00 to 5:00 P.M. (closed weekends September through May). Some tours require a fee.

Insider Tip Camping is available in several locations between Cimarron and Eagle Nest on US 64 within **Cimarron Canyon State Park.** Tall, 40-million-year-old granite formations along the riverbanks—dubbed the Palisades Sill—have made this a favorite with climbers. If you like trout-fishing, look no further.

13 *Best* Volcano

From the thousand-foot peak of **Capulín Volcano**, on a clear day, you can see parts of five states: New Mexico, Colorado, Kansas, Texas, and Oklahoma. An almost perfectly shaped cone, this curiosity was created 10,000 years ago (practically yesterday in geo-logical time). So "recent" was the last eruption, in fact, that experts consider this a dormant volcano, not an extinct one. Nevertheless, visitors are invited to walk brazenly *into* the Capulín crater (more properly called a caldera) for a closer look. The self-guided rim trail is about a mile long. You can drive to the top of the volcano and hike from there.

"From the summit of Capulín, you can see several nearby mesas capped with lava," notes geologist Mike Kashuba, who has studied the area. "All the land one sees around these high points was once the same height, but the lava capstone has prevented erosion on the mesas." The 40-mile-wide mountain about 10 miles to the southeast, Sierra Grande, constitutes the remains of a shield volcano believed to form the largest peak in North America that is not part of a mountain range. It rises some 2,200 feet above the surrounding terrain.

If You Go: **Capulín Volcano National Monument (278-2201)** is reached by driving 30 miles east of Ratón on US 64/87, then 3 miles north on NM 325 from the village of Capulín. The visitors' center is open from 8:00 A.M. to 4:30 P.M. (until 8:00 P.M. during summer). Admission is $3 per car. There's no camping, but picnic tables and restrooms are available. The volcano's name comes from the Spanish word for the chokecherry tree, which grows wild on its slopes.

14 *Best* String of Lakes

Three of the prettiest lakes in New Mexico are found at **Sugarite Canyon State Park,** near the Colorado border northeast of Ratón. Unlike many New Mexico lakes, these are surrounded by magnificent mountains, meadows, wildflowers, and forests.

"What a gem of a park it is!" exclaimed Las Vegas–based columnist Art Latham in the Santa Fe newspaper *New Mexican.* "[Sugarite] is a cool, generously watered retreat."

Stocked with fish and ringed with the campsites of the Soda Pocket Campground, Maloya, Dorothy, and Alice Lakes are small, quiet, and perfect for sailboats. Keep an eye out and you may see deer, elk, mountain lion, bobcat, beaver, or bear, all plentiful in the area.

"This is the best place to go to see fall colors," says leaf-peeper Elizabeth McNitt, a Santa Fe painter. "My husband and I try to visit in late September or early October, when foliage is usually changing."

As you drive here you'll pass old coal mines around the ghost town of Sugarite, abandoned since 1941, and a turn-of-the-century resort that never opened because its British owner skipped town. Just over the Colorado line is the **Sugarite Ski Basin,** accessible only through New Mexico.

If You Go: **Sugarite State Park (445-5607)** is 11 miles northeast of Ratón via NM 72 and NM 526. There's a $3-per-carload day-use fee and an additional fee for camping.

15 *Best* Place to Scuba Dive

Surely you jest … scuba-diving in New Mexico? It *can* be done, although the **Blue Hole** near Santa Rosa is one of your only options.

"And definitely the best," declares Rita Cadena, a longtime New Mexico resident who has dived the Blue Hole. The "hole" is a deep, natural well filled with artesian water filtered through underground limestone and sandstone deposits. The water here is so clear and the setting so unusual that scuba divers from throughout the United States come to explore the crystalline pool. Sixty feet across and 81 feet deep—deep enough to warrant "open water" certification—the Blue Hole nevertheless teems with a wide variety of fish, snails, and aquatic plant life. The water replaces itself every six hours at a rate of 3,000 gallons per minute and remains a constant 61°F year-round.

The Blue Hole is only five minutes from downtown Santa Rosa. In fact, it is *owned* by the city of Santa Rosa, along with several other small lakes (notably Park Lake and James Wallace Lake) that make excellent summer swimming destinations. You need a permit from the city's police department ($10) in order to dive at the Blue Hole, verifying that you're PADI-certified or accompanied by a certified instructor. It's best to visit on a weekday, since the Hole can get fairly crowded on Saturday and Sunday (many scuba classes come here from throughout New Mexico to train students). There are many motels and restaurants in the area or you can camp at the Blue Hole itself. No permit is required for snorkeling or swimming.

If You Go: **Santa Rosa** is 114 miles east of Albuquerque on I-40. The **Blue Hole** is less than a mile from the city center on NM 91. You can get air tanks filled at the nearby Santa Rosa Dive Shop. **Chamber of Commerce information: 472-3763.**

16 *Best* Buddy Holly Memorabilia

The **Norman Petty Studio** on **Seventh Street** in Clovis contains relics of recording sessions here involving Buddy Holly, Roy Orbison, and other rock stars who were born and raised along the New Mexico–Texas border and recorded their first music here. The best time to visit is during the **Clovis Music Festival,** held every midsummer, during which the Buddy Holly Memorial Society meets and the **Rock 'n' Roll Hot-Air Balloon Rally** sends gasbags into the sky. There are also street dances, a parade, fifties-era car show, community picnic, and concerts at Petty's Main Street Studio Auditorium.

"Old-timers who knew Holly, Orbison, and the Big Bopper tell stories and share their private recordings from rock's early days," says Mike Pitel, an analyst for New Mexico's Department of Tourism. "You can even sing along to the greatest hits of the fifties and sixties."

If You Go: Call the **Clovis Chamber of Commerce (763-3435)** for information on the music festival and balloon rally. For a **Norm Petty Studio** tour, call its Portales-based manager, Kenneth Broad, at least 24 hours in advance at **356-6422.** Clovis is 60 miles south of I-40 via NM 209 and 9 miles west of the Texas border via US 70/84.

Insider Tip If you're in the area during the summer months, check out *The Real Billy the Kid,* a historical drama performed outdoors Saturday and Sunday evenings at the **Caprock Amphitheater (576-2455),** 49 miles north of Clovis near San Jon. The high plains setting is spectacular and a barbecue dinner is available.

17 Best Tribute to the Navajo People

Bosque Redondo, at **Fort Sumner State Monument,** commemorates a particularly shameful episode in U.S. history that occurred in this farming area along the Pecos River. Federal authorities under the leadership of Kit Carson in 1862 forcibly relocated nearly 7,000 "hostile" Navajo Indians from their homelands in northwestern New Mexico and eastern Arizona and marched them 400 miles (the "Long Walk") to the U.S. Army's Fort Sumner, where Bosque Redondo was established as a Native American concentration camp. Officials felt that by relocating the Navajo, they could be controlled and converted into "civilized" farmers.

The plan was a miserable failure. The Navajo, a nomadic tribe unaccustomed to (and uninterested in) farming, were plagued by drought, disease, and insects. In 1868, after the Indians refused to plant crops, the government conceded defeat and signed a treaty granting the Navajo sovereignty over what became the largest Indian reservation in the United States. The dispossessed survivors straggled home, ending their forced exile on foot.

"Although the old fort and adjacent encampment have disappeared, some of the thousands of cottonwood trees planted by my people remain along the banks of the Pecos," notes Eve Benally, a community services coordinator for the Navajo Nation. "Our presence here is not forgotten."

A memorial beneath these old cottonwoods has been erected by the modern Navajo to honor their ancestors, 3,000 of whom died here. Each June, representatives of the Navajo Nation return to Bosque Redondo carrying large rocks from their reservation. These are reverently added to a pile that represents the Navajo homeland, in a deliberate exile that benefits the spirits of the Navajo who are buried near the site. (About 500 Mescalero Apache were imprisoned at Bosque Redondo at the same time as the Navajo, but they managed to escape after three years.)

Separate from this shrine is the nearby **Fort Sumner Museum and Visitors' Center,** where exhibits describe the function of the fort and reservation, as well as the killing of Billy the Kid here by

Sheriff Pat Garrett. The Kid's grave is nearby in a small cemetery next to a private museum. The museum is small and overpriced, but it's interesting to see the famous outlaw's final resting place. Billy's tombstone is fenced and tied down to prevent people from stealing and holding it for ransom—which has happened twice. This has prompted residents of the nearby town to hold a **World's Richest Tombstone Race** each June during their **Fort Sumner Days** celebration.

If You Go: **Fort Sumner** is 47 miles southeast of Santa Rosa on US 60/ 84. The **state monument (355-2573)** is 8 miles south of town on NM 272 and open from 8:30 A.M. to 5:00 P.M. Thursday through Monday for a $2 admission. There's no camping, but plenty of restaurants and motels are nearby. You can picnic on the shady grounds near the memorial.

Chapter 8
Las Cruces and Southwestern New Mexico

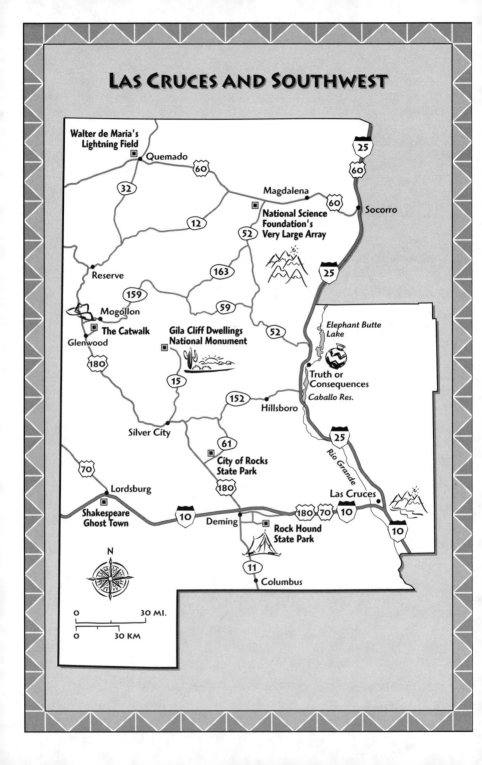

LAS CRUCES AND SOUTHWEST

What's Best about Las Cruces and Southwestern New Mexico

*D*espite its status as the state's second-biggest city, Las Cruces is largely ignored as a travel destination. In outlying parts of the state many know Las Cruces primarily as the home of New Mexico's land-grant university and sometimes jokingly call it "little El Paso." Yet there's much more to this community of more than 75,000 residents. And its location and services make it an ideal staging area for further explorations of the southwest quadrant.

Rich in history, Las Cruces ("the crosses") was named by the Spanish to commemorate a caravan of travelers massacred here by Apache Indians during the early 1800s while en route from Taos to Mexico. Those who died were buried under a field of simple crosses. Later, a village was established that helped supply nearby Fort Seldon and other military camps that protected trade routes. Now in ruins, Seldon was the boyhood home of General Douglas MacArthur (his father commanded the fort during the 1880s) and a posting for "buffalo soldiers" of the nineteenth century: African-Americans who helped tame the West. The adjacent village of La Mesilla was briefly the capital of the Confederate territory of Arizona and for three centuries served as a hub of the vigorous trade network with Mexico. In 1853 the Gadsden Purchase was signed in La Mesilla, shifting New Mexico's boundaries to their current coordinates.

Today Las Cruces is an important agricultural and engineering research center, home to New Mexico State University. The Río Grande, which flows through the city, irrigates thousands of acres of Mesilla Valley alfalfa, chile, cotton, and pecans. Cattle ranching and high-tech military research are also important industries, with many residents commuting to work at nearby White Sands Missile Range and Fort Bliss.

Beyond Las Cruces, southwestern New Mexico is lightly populated, with not many more residents than when Butterfield stagecoaches first trundled through in 1858. The warm, tawny deserts are barren and stark, punctuated by cool, forested mountains—both contain remarkably diverse flora and fauna. The Gila Mountain Wilderness, in particular, is a magnificent wonderland of nature. It was here that essayist/forest ranger Aldo Leopold made his successful plea for establishing a formal wilderness system that now extends throughout the United States.

"Sunsets here are stunning," wrote environmentalist Dave Foreman, an EarthFirst! founder and New Mexico native, in *The Big Outside.* "There is a striking starkness about the land. ... The spell this land casts is subtle, subliminal."

Southwestern New Mexico, like the rest of the state, is a place of dramatic contrasts and sweeping vistas, where artifacts of ancient history are found next to society's latest technological marvels. Here a diversity of cultural traditions and languages—coupled with a mild climate—yield a refreshingly friendly and tolerant group of people.

As elsewhere in the state, the most practical way to get around southwestern New Mexico is by car. If this is your primary destination, you can fly to El Paso and be in Las Cruces within an hour. Driving time from Albuquerque to Las Cruces via I-25 is about four and a half hours.

1 *Best* Enchilada Festival

Early every October, thousands of Las Cruces residents turn out to cook (and eat) the world's biggest enchilada, sometimes more than 7 feet in width. It's part of the **Whole Enchilada Festival,** a three-day fall harvest celebration of the chile peppers that are an essential ingredient of this and other New Mexican dishes. Based in the downtown mall on Main Street, this culinary extravaganza affords visitors a chance to buy local arts and crafts, dance in the street, meet new friends, and generally make merry—as well as sample the largest enchilada on the planet.

"This is a really fun event for children and adults alike, particularly those who enjoy spicy food," says Katharine Kagel, owner of Santa Fe's Café Pasqual's, an inspired consumer of New Mexico chile. "Remember my motto, *'panza llena, corazon contento'*—'full stomach, full heart.'"

Runner-up in this category is the **Hatch Chile Festival,** held in early September at the Hatch Airport. You'll see a chile-themed parade and prizes given for the biggest, hottest, and best chiles. You can buy your own fresh chiles (most experts agree that Hatch produces the best in the United States), *ristras* (strings of dried chiles), powdered chile, and related products.

If You Go: Las Cruces is at the junction of I-25 (north-south) and I-10 (east-west), about 225 miles south of Albuquerque and 40 miles northwest of El Paso, Texas. The **Las Cruces Convention and Visitors Bureau** answers at **800-FIESTAS.** For information on the **Hatch Chile Festival,** call **267-4847.** Hatch is in the heart of prime chile-growing territory, 37 miles north of Las Cruces on I-25.

Insider Tip The **Las Cruces Downtown Mall on Main Street** is the site of the deservedly popular **Farmers and Crafts Market,** held every Wednesday and Saturday throughout the year. You'll find local produce, baked good, arts, and crafts. At the north end of the mall sits an 1879 log cabin, moved here from nearby mountains and decorated with period furnishings.

2 *Best* Breakfast

Nellie's Café is an old-fashioned diner recommended by Las Cruces locals for its home-style New Mexican breakfasts, which include lots of local chile. Open daily (except Sunday) from 8:00 A.M. to 8:00 P.M. Lunch and dinner are also very fine: try the tostada compuesto and carne adovada. Another popular standby is **Pancake Alley,** open daily from 5:30 A.M. to 9:00 P.M. and specializing in an amazing variety of pancakes.

If You Go: Nellie's (524-9982) is at **1226 West Hadley** and **Pancake Alley (527-0087)** at **2147 West Picacho.** The former is not to be confused with Little Nellie's, which has a different owner and less interesting cuisine.

3 𝓑est Lunch

Elsa, a Las Cruces native who'd rather not divulge her last name since she's recently made it big in show biz, recommends the "incredibly inexpensive" and *que sabrosa* New Mexican cuisine at **Chope's,** a bar and café on the "old road" to El Paso. This is a fun, homey place open daily for lunch and dinner. Warning: the chile-laced dishes are hot as hell.

The consensus among locals is that the best hamburgers in Las Cruces are served at **Henry J's,** located in an old converted house on Idaho, off El Paseo. Burgers are all they serve—but what burgers! (Bring your appetite.)

In Old Mesilla, a unique and recommended choice is **Peppers** (in a historic hacienda on the plaza), with a menu that includes Mexican wontons, spit-roasted chicken, blue-corn catfish, seafood chimichangas, and banana enchiladas (!) for dessert. Next door, sharing the same building and owner, is the more elegant (and more expensive) **Double Eagle,** with fine continental entrées and a lavish salad bar. Linking the two is a lush outdoor patio, where food from both restaurants is served. "It's worth going for the ambiance," says one longtime customer, "and the food is pretty good—particularly the tried-and-true dishes."

If You Go: **Chope's (233-3420)** is 16 miles south of Las Cruces on NM 28: drive through shady pecan orchards until you reach the farming town of La Mesa. **Henry J's (525-2211)** is at **523 Idaho Avenue. Peppers (523-4999)** and the **Double Eagle (523-6700)** are on the east side of the historic Old Mesilla Plaza. For another taste treat, take a free tour of **Stahlmann Farms (800-654-6887),** 12 miles south of Las Cruces on NM 28 and one of the world's largest producers of pecan nuts.

4 Best Dinner

Carrillo's is the favorite dining spot of Las Cruces native and NMSU alumnus Mike Chappell, along with many other discriminating New Mexicans.

"The chile is just hot enough and the flavor is superb," says Chappell, who recommends a lunch plate of flat enchiladas topped with red chile and a fried egg. An aesthetic bonus is the lovely *santo* painting of La Reina del Valle that hangs behind the cash register.

Possibly the most renowned restaurant in the region is **La Posta,** housed in a former Butterfield stage stop on the Old Mesilla Plaza. The adobe was constructed around 1820 and has been remodeled into a very pleasant dining space. House specialties are steaks and New Mexican cuisine. The crowd at La Posta is rather touristy and the food rather bland, but prices are moderate. Better food and a nicer setting can be found at the nearby **Mesón de Mesilla**—also the area's best place to spend the night. Surrounded by beautiful gardens, this B&B boasts a swimming pool, bicycles, and horseshoe pit for guest use.

"The best restaurant of all in Las Cruces is **Tatsu**," declares Lynn Nusom, a food critic, cookbook author, and syndicated TV chef who lives in nearby Hillsboro. "It serves wonderful Japanese cuisine—I heartily recommend the ginger beef and the California rolls."

If You Go: **Carrillo's (523-9913)** is located behind the Welcome Inn in downtown Las Cruces, at Amador and Main. **La Posta (524-3524)** is on the southeast corner of the plaza in Old Mesilla, **Mesón de Mesilla (525-9212)** at **1803 Avenida de Mesilla (NM 28)**, and **Tatsu (526-7144)** at **930 El Paseo Road.** Another recommended place to spend the night is **Lundeen Inn of the Arts (526-3327)** at **618 South Alameda.** This B&B combines the owners' art gallery and architectural studio within a historic adobe hacienda.

5 Best Duck Race

Robert W. Duck—yes, that's his real name—is the owner of Deming's winningest ducks.

"My birds have won 12 out of 16 annual races," says Duck, a poultry farmer from Bosque Farms. "But they did so well that in 1995 the organizers decided to exclude professional trainers like me from the competition—they said it would be more fun if everybody competed as amateurs."

Tucked into the state's southwest corner, Deming hosts the **Great American Duck Race** each year on the fourth weekend of August. The community's chamber of commerce tongue-in-cheek slogan, in fact, is: "The Home of Pure Artesian Water and Fast Ducks."

Race-week festivities include a tortilla toss, outhouse race, red and green chile cook-off, wild cow milking contest, kids' calf scramble, golf tournament, hot-air balloon rally, car show, arts-and-crafts fair, rodeo, parade, and, yes, a big silly duck race. Entrants choose a duck from dozens provided by the local chamber of commerce and cheer their fowl on during competition at the regional fairgrounds. Dances, food booths, and the crowning of a "Duck Queen" and "Best-dressed Duck" round out the event. The duck derby was conceived in 1979 in a bar (where else!) as a way of drumming up visitor interest in remote Luna County. It seems to work … at least for one week.

Deming's lodging isn't fancy and the best restaurant is downtown's showy **Si Señor,** a family-owned New Mexico chain that also has outlets in Las Cruces and Alamogordo. "They have really good, hot Mexican dishes," says food critic Lynn Nusom, a confessed chile addict.

If You Go: Deming is 60 miles west of Las Cruces and on I-10, or 46 miles southwest of Hatch on NM 26. The **Chamber of Commerce (800-848-4955)** is at **800 East Pine, Si Señor (546-3938)** at **200 East Pine.**

Insider Tip The **Deming–Luna Mimbres Museum (546-2382)** at **301 South Silver** is the best cultural repository in southern New Mexico, with an impressive array of Mimbres Indian artifacts dating back 2,000 years. There is also a large collection of old quilts and dolls. The brick building housing the museum has an interesting history of its own. It was constructed as an armory shortly after Mexican revolutionary Pancho Villa's famous raid on nearby **Columbus,** when there was widespread fear that Deming might also be attacked by Villa and his well-armed followers. Open Monday through Saturday from 9:00 A.M. to 4:00 P.M. and Sundays 1:30 to 4:00 P.M. with no admission charge. The villa raid commemorated in Columbus at Pancho Villa State Park.

6 *Best* Park for Rock Hounds

Where else are visitors not merely allowed but encouraged to *take home* part of the environment?

You can legally load your trunk with up to 20 pounds of jasper, agate, quartz crystals, onyx, black perlite, and opal samples at 240-acre **Rock Hound State Park,** tucked in the Little Florida Mountains near Deming. Kids of all ages particularly enjoy busting open "thunder eggs," a type of spherulite that contains swirls of agate and opal inside.

"Try to avoid summer visits as it gets insufferably hot," advises Anne Griffin, an amateur rock hound who frequents the area. "Even if you have no serious interest in rock collecting, you'll find lots of pretty rocks, particu-

Trail signs at Rock Hound State Park.

larly in shades of red and brown." Griffin says true aficionados will want to come in early March to coincide with the annual **Rock Hound Roundup (546-9281)** held at the Deming Fairgrounds.

Runner-up: Another good place in the "we love rocks" category is the nearby **City of Rocks State Park.** This is a curious middle-of-nowhere landscape of tall, weirdly shaped volcanic tuff. Children will love to climb among the monoliths, formed by nearby eruptions millions of years ago and subsequently eroded by wind, rain, and snow. Avoid Easter weekend, which is notoriously crowded.

If You Go: Rock Hound State Park is about 8 miles southeast of Deming off NM 11 on Palomas Road **(546-1212).** There's a $3 per car admission to the park, open daily from 7:30 A.M. to sunset. Amenities include a campground with showers, RV hookups, hiking trails, and a playground. Two miles south is **Spring Canyon Park,** a desert oasis in the Big Florida Mountains that has picnic and camping facilities. If you're lucky, you may catch a glimpse of the Persian ibex, an exotic animal introduced here during the 1970s as a target for big game hunters.

City of Rocks (536-2800) is 28 miles northwest of Deming on NM 61 Open daily, 7:00 A.M. to sunset, for a $3 per vehicle fee. There are camping and picnic facilities, plus a cactus garden, playground, and restrooms with showers.

7 *Best* Privately Owned Ghost Town

Shakespeare, an abandoned community 2 miles outside the village of Lordsburg, has been painstakingly preserved by its private owners to offer modern-day visitors a realistic sense of what the life of a 19th-century silver miner was like. Close your eyes and picture Johnny Ringo and Curly Bill Brocius treading the parched streets in search of poker buddies and bawdy house girls. Members of the Hill family (who bought the entire town in 1935) conduct regular tours of their old hotel, saloon, stagecoach stop, and other attractions, plus reenactments of historical events. Call ahead for a schedule.

At one time about 3,000 people lived in Shakespeare, but the town has been virtually deserted since the 1930s, when the silver ore played out and railroad traffic shifted north.

Another ghost town in the area worth visiting is **Steins** (pronounced "Steens"), 20 miles west of **Lordsburg** and 3 miles east of the Arizona state line. There's a small fee for tours, although you can see much of Steins for free simply by looking out your car window as you zip along I-10.

If You Go: Shakespeare (542-9034) is reached via Exit 22 from I-10 at Lordsburg. Admission is $3, tours are generally offered on weekends only. **Steins (542-9791)** is off Exit 3 from I-10. Located 23 miles east of the Arizona state line, **Lordsburg** itself is unexciting, although there are plenty of places to eat and spend the night. Across from the old train station you'll find a tourist information center and the best espresso and cappuccino in town, cheerfully dispensed in an electronic repair shop. The best Mexican food is at 24-hour **El Charro (542-3400)** at **3209 SP Boulevard.**

Insider Tip "Head south from Lordsburg on NM 8 and you enter the state's boot heel," notes Mike Pitel of New Mexico's tourism department. "This area contains some of the Southwest's emptiest and most pristine desert wilderness, with flora and fauna found nowhere else in the United States." Eventually, via unpaved NM 81, you'll reach the Mexican border at Antelope Wells. For a unique dining experience, stop at **Willie's Nightmare Café** in tiny **Animas** for a cold soda, a hot hamburger, and maybe a chat with a real live cowboy. The sunsets in this part of the state are especially magnificent, seeming to linger for hours above the horizon.

8 *Best* Cliff Dwellings

Gila Cliff Dwellings National Monument is the ancient home of a little-known group of Indians who abandoned the remote site roughly six centuries ago. Some 42 rooms in a sandstone escarpment were inhabited during the fourteenth century by members of the Mogollon tribe, who hunted and fished in the nearby mountains. It's unclear why they chose to live in such an isolated location or why they disappeared from the area around A.D. 1400. In later years, this area was a stronghold for the nomadic Apache, the last tribe to be subdued by the U.S. military. The cliff dwellings were not discovered by non-Indians until the 1880s.

The structures are tucked into a cluster of five natural caves among the cliffs, which are surrounded by beautiful pine forest. Trails extend for miles into the surrounding Gila Mountains.

"Thanks to forest ranger Aldo Leopold's untiring efforts, in 1924 this became the first congressionally designated wilderness," notes biologist Charlie Luthin. "You can either set off to explore the area on foot, or arrange with local outfitters for a horse, mule, or llama."

There are many natural hot springs in the vicinity, the nearest of which is accessible by a short hike up the middle fork of the Gila River from the forest service's visitors' center. Three miles southeast of the monument on NM 15 is the **Gila Hot Springs Vacation Center,** which offers groceries, camping, RV hookups, cabins, wilderness outfitting, and access to a hot spring. Kids enjoy the **Faerie Land Museum's** collection of miniature towns and dolls. Nearby is the Grapevine Campground—which claims to have the world's largest grapevine—and the **Heart Bar Wildlife Area,** where the Department of Game and Fish studies mountain lions and develops elk herds.

If You Go: **Gila Cliff Dwellings National Monument (536-9461)** is 46 miles north of Silver City at the end of NM 15. The paved two-lane road is very twisty, so allow at least two hours each way from Silver City. The best plan is to set aside a full day for a trip to the park. Hours are 8:00 A.M. to 6:00 P.M., with earlier closing during the off-season. The visitors' center has helpful exhibits to explain the cliff dwellings, which are about 0.5 mile away by car and yet another mile by trail. The monument's Scorpion Campground is run by the National Forest Service, which is also in charge of the surrounding 3 million acres.

Insider Tip A good base for an excursion is **Silver City,** located in the foothills of "the Gila" at the intersection of four state highways. As the name implies, this is an old silver-mining town—now twice reborn, first as a retreat for tuberculosis victims and more recently as an intriguing community of students (attending Western New Mexico University), cattle ranchers (the biggest agricultural enterprise hereabouts), copper miners (Phelps-Dodge's huge **Santa Rita open-pit copper mine** is about 15 miles to the east), and retirees (including many refugees from California). These disparate groups come together every mid-October for the **Cielo Encantado Kite Fiesta.**

Silver City is distinguished by its well-preserved Victorian-era architecture, including many homes with hand-carved woodwork and handsome Italianate mansard roofs. The **Silver City Museum and Gift Shop** is in a converted residence (**312 West Broadway**) that is a classic example of Victorian finery.

Accommodations include **The Palace B&B,** a charming hotel built as a bank in 1882 and now fully restored. **The Palace (388-1811)** is at **106 West Broadway.** An Edwardian mansion called the **Carter House (388-5485)** is also in the historic district at **101 North Cooper Street.** It has five private rooms and a dorm-style youth hostel downstairs. (The owner, Lucy Ditworth, operates another B&B near the village of San Lorenzo, in the Mimbres Valley east of Silver City.)

Three miles outside Silver City, the 160-acre **Bear Mountain Guest Ranch (538-2538)** is a 15-room B&B that also arranges nature, fishing, bicycling, horseback-riding, and archaeology tours. The owner is a vivacious and well-informed woman who leads nature treks throughout the area.

9 *Best* Catwalk

Don't be confused by your map. The **Mogollon Catwalk** is *not* in Mogollon. It's actually 5 miles east of Glenwood, some 17 circuitous miles by car from the curious ghost town of Mogollon.

The catwalk consists of a narrow, metal passageway that clings to the near-vertical cliffs of spectacular Whitewater Canyon. This unusual structure was built in 1893 to maintain a suspended water pipeline to a nearby mill that, in turn, provided hydroelectric power to the local mining industry. Workers used the catwalk to repair the pipes, some still visible. After falling into disuse shortly after the turn of the century, the scaffolding was upgraded for tourism purposes during the 1930s. It now hugs the side of the gorge about 20 feet above the streambed, along sheer cliffs that tower up to 1,400 feet overhead. Needless to say, this experience isn't for everyone.

"The steel mesh catwalk is well-maintained and has a guardrail, but those with a fear of heights may not want to hike along it," advises Beth Miller, a ranger with the National Forest Service, which administers the area. "Others should find it exciting and dramatic. I wouldn't recommend *anybody* following the catwalk at night, however."

The catwalk's namesake is very much worth a visit. The hills around **Mogollon**—current population 17—produced more than $20 million worth of gold, silver, and copper during a late-nineteenth-century boom. Even Butch Cassidy and the Sundance Kid worked the rich veins here. Nothing much happened after they left until 1973, when the Henry Fonda movie *My Name Is Nobody* was filmed here and some of the old structures were fixed up— only to fall apart again. Mogollon's main street and sidewalks are angled along the steep banks of Silver Creek and you must cross narrow wooden bridges to get to most of the buildings. During the summer months a museum is open, along with several galleries and cafés. The town's most unusual store sells model trains and Christmas ornaments year-round. Mogollon is 9 miles east of Alma on NM 159. Turn off US 180 and follow the twisting road into the mountains.

If You Go: Glenwood is 63 miles northwest of Silver City via US 180. To reach the 1.1-mile-long **catwalk,** head east on NM 174 (Catwalk Road) until it dead-ends at a shady picnic area. There is no admission charge at these unattended sites. A wilderness trailhead is at the upper end of the walkway and you can also hike from (or to) the catwalk via the steep Trail 41 from a posted parking area on NM 159.

Insider Tip Continue east and you'll pass through some of the least inhabited and most beautiful terrain in New Mexico. There are a couple of simple campgrounds but no other services for 135 miles. Be prepared! This stretch of NM 159 is unpaved and not recommended for large RVs or vehicles pulling trailers. It's usually closed from November through March due to mud and snow.

Nearby accommodations include Glenwood's **Los Olmos Guest Ranch (539-2311),** at the intersection of US 180 and NM 174. This B&B, which features 13 rock cabins, a swimming pool, and hot tub, is closed in winter. There are a couple of year-round motels and restaurants in Glenwood and its mercantile sells gas and groceries.

10 *Best* Place to Watch an Electrical Storm

Unless you're keen on hunting and fishing—both popular pastimes in the area—there's not much reason to spend time in the tiny village of Quemado.

One exception is a prearranged visit to **Walter de María's Lightning Field,** a unique and large-scale piece of environmental art located on a high-desert plain about 20 miles from Quemado. (The owners have asked that the exact location not be revealed, since visitors are only allowed by reservation through a booking office in Albuquerque.)

De María's creation consists of 400 shiny, pointed stainless steel poles, placed at 220-foot intervals in a rectangular grid that measures one mile by 3,330 feet. The height of each shiny pole varies from about 15 to 21 feet so that the top of this six-acre bed of nails appears perfectly flat. During thunderstorms the poles attract lightning strikes in a dazzling display. Best odds are during July and August. In case you're worried, there's no danger of being hit by a lightning bolt during a thunderstorm here as long as you stay indoors. Each pole is grounded.

"It's meditation. It's solitude. It's electric," declares writer Sarah Lovett, who finds inspiration here for writing such thrillers as *Dangerous Attachments.* "It's wonderful when lightning strikes, but even when it doesn't the field still offers an incredible light show as peach and violet sun rays reflect off the poles ... It's really the silence of this place that's astounding—the quiet that's part of open spaces."

Visitors pay a fee (well in advance) to stay in a renovated 1930s homesteader's cabin near the field. Food (cooked by you) and transportation from Quemado are included in the price. A small museum in Quemado explains how the Lightning Field was constructed (1971–77) and displays dramatic photos taken during lightning storms. De Maria searched for five years through six Western states before he picked this spot, chosen for its open, flat ground, high elevation (7,200 feet), and relatively high incidence of lightning. It's forbidden to take photos at the site, but you can buy slides and postcards at the museum.

If You Go: For information regarding **The Lightning Field,** call **989-5602** or write **2 Wind NW, Albuquerque, NM 87120.** Quemado is on US 60, 45 miles west of Datil and 33 miles east of the Arizona border. There are several restaurants and motels in Quemado—none noteworthy. Man-made Quemado Lake, 18 miles south on NM 32, is a popular destination for trout-fishing and there's a campground nearby.

11 *Best* Astronomical Observatory

Speaking of lightning, the **National Science Foundation's Very Large Array** is "a very striking place," observes Jerry Hoogerwerf, a charter pilot and manager of the Socorro Municipal Airport. Indeed, for travelers approaching the site on US 60, says Hoogerwerf, "It really looks like something from another planet—with or without an electrical storm."

The Very Large Array.

The interplanetary connection is not far off. The Very Large Array is a highly sophisticated research center for the study of radio waves emanating from energy sources (such as stars) scattered throughout distant parts of the universe. It consists of dozens of enormous, 235-ton satellite-type dishes, all mounted on railroad cars that travel on steel tracks. Working together, these 27 dishes form a single antenna—the world's most powerful and sensitive radio telescope—used to map regions of space that are too far away to be detected by even the world's best optical telescopes.

How far away are the energy sources being monitored by the VLA? Some signals are believed to be waves formed by the so-called Big Bang, which many scientists consider the birth of our universe. If so, the emissions being picked up here are coming from nearly six trillion miles away.

Although the VLA is not supposed to be a listening post for UFOs, if there is any sort of radio or TV station on another planet it will probably be picked up here first. So far, E.T. isn't talking. The site was chosen because of its flatness and isolation: an absence of potentially interfering water vapor and electromagnetic radiation is needed in order to listen clearly to outer space.

If You Go: The **Very Large Array (772-4255)** covers several square miles in the Plains of San Agustín, a flat, wide valley bisected by US 60 about 40 miles west of Socorro. There is a small but excellent self-guided visitors' center (open daily from 8:00 A.M. to sunset) where you can view displays that explain the basic operations of the observatory. More detailed explanations are found in a booklet on sale for $3. There is no admission charge to the VLA and you can walk right up to an 82-foot-diameter dish or, if you're lucky, watch it being moved along the railroad tracks. There is a picnic area and interpretive trail at the visitors' center. Guests aren't allowed to climb the dishes, enter the buildings, or leave designated pathways.

12 *Best* Old-Timers' Festival

The beauty pageant at Magdalena's annual **Old-Timers' Festival** has some unusual guidelines. The Festival Queen, for example, must be at least 60 years old. The lovely lass who wins is paraded through the streets of Magdalena in a horse-drawn carriage. There's a special rodeo for gray-hairs, too, along with the requisite barbecue and Western dance. You'll note that many of the participants in these events wear period costumes from the turn of the century, when Magdalena had triple its current population of 300.

Held in early July each year, the Old-Timers' Festival is a kind of town-wide family reunion, in which hundreds of people who were born and raised here (but now live elsewhere) return to renew ties with neighbors, relatives, and friends, many of them also Magdalena "expatriates."

Originally a mining town (gold, silver, and lead), Magdalena grew in importance after a railroad spur linked it to Socorro in 1885. Local cattle and sheep ranchers used this railhead until the tracks were abandoned a half-century later. It's said that Magdalena was once the biggest livestock shipping point west of Chicago, but today the town is slowly fading away. The name, incidentally, refers to a nearby rock formation said to resemble the head of Mary Magdalene. The town was said to be immune to Apache raids because of the protective influence of this image.

If You Go: Magdalena is 27 miles west of Socorro on US 60 (at the intersection of NM 169) in the foothills of the Magdalena Mountains. **Old-Timers' Festival** information: **835-0424.** There are a couple of motels, restaurants, grocery stores, and antique shops, as well as a post office.

Insider Tip About 3 miles south of Magdalena is the ghost town of **Kelly,** once a thriving mining community (witness the abandoned house and smelter foundations) that became totally uninhabited after nearby lead and smithsonite deposits played out. At its peak in the 1880s, Kelly had seven saloons and two churches, one of which (the Catholic chapel) is still in occasional use. The town is privately owned, but if you sign a liability release (available on site) you're welcome to poke around. The turnoff to Kelly from US 60 is NM 107, west of the forest service station.

13 *Best* Indoor Hot Springs

Truth or Consequences—"T or C," as the locals call it—may be the only town in the world renamed in order to promote a game show. It was known until 1950 as Hot Springs, after the natural thermal springs found along this stretch of the Río Grande. To learn more, check out the local museum's **Ralph Edwards Room,** detailing the story of how Edwards, host of the radio (later TV) quiz show *Truth or Consequences* launched a national contest that led to Hot Springs changing its name on the program's tenth anniversary. Early each May the now-retired emcee returns for a parade and fiesta honoring this momentous occasion. (In 1970 the town's voters rejected a proposal to change the name back to Hot

Springs.) Every October there is also a commemoration of the town's pre-Edwards history during **Geronimo Days.**

T or C's geothermal waters now are all enclosed and visitors must pay an hourly fee to use them. One exception is a 115°F sacred spring where the famous Apache leader Geronimo is said to have relaxed: it's now a city park.

The best of the several private spas operating in this small town is the **Artesian Bathhouse and Travel Court,** according to Ann Muriel, a school nurse who has come here often to soak her weary body in the calming waters.

"It's clean, inexpensive, and well maintained," says Muriel, who recommends the Artesian to friends, family, and clients. "The waters are very soothing and healing." The main mineral found in these waters is sodium chloride (common table salt) but there are also substantial concentrations of calcium, magnesium, and potassium. Many people swear by the minerals' presumed healthful properties.

If You Go: The **Artesian Bathhouse (894-2684)** is at **312 Marr Street,** near the center of Truth or Consequences. Open daily (except Wednesday and the month of August) from 7:00 A.M. to 7:00 P.M. Private tubs (more like small indoor wading pools) are rented for $6 an hour double-occupancy ($3 single). Children under six are free, ages seven to twelve are $1, and adults over 65 pay $2. Besides trailers, the park accommodates RVs and pickup campers. If the Artesian is booked up, try the **Sierra Grande Health Spa** at **501 McAdoo (894-6976)** or the **Charles Motel and Bathhouse** at **701 Broadway (894-7154).**

Truth or Consequences is 75 miles north of Las Cruces on I-25. **La Cocina (894-6200)** at **1400 North Date,** is known for its New Mexican dishes. Besides Ralph Edwards memorabilia (including videos of the *Truth or Consequences* TV show), the **Geronimo Springs Museum (894-6600)** at **325 Main Street** displays a collection of exquisite Mimbres Indian pottery. It's open daily from 9:00 A.M. to 5:00 P.M. with a $2 admission. T or C has a large number of antique and secondhand stores, plus one of New Mexico's biggest cactus nurseries: **Buffalo Bill's (894-0790)** at **1600 South Broadway.**

Visitors on the shores of Elephant Butte Lake.

For those who like boating, fishing, and swimming, New Mexico's largest lake (43 miles long) is a few miles north of Truth or Consequences. Created as an irrigation and flood-control measure in 1916, **Elephant Butte Lake** has a **marina (744-5486)** and stores where boats and tackle can be rented, as does **Caballo Lake,** a smaller reservoir several miles south of T or C. Both lakes are state parks and have camping and RV sites. Anglers will find plenty of pike, carp, catfish, and bass.

14 *Best* Revived Ghost Towns

Tucked in the rolling foothills of the Black Range, the semi-ghost town of Hillsboro comes to life the first weekend of September with an **Apple Festival** that celebrates one of the smallest—but sweetest—such crops in New Mexico. There are street dances, food booths, art exhibits, and, as you'd expect, apples prepared every which way. Founded in 1877, Hillsboro was one of several area mining towns that faded by the end of the nineteenth century. Today it's kept alive by a group of writers, artists, filmmakers, and merchants who favor its unusual combination of solitude and scenery. There are a couple of art galleries, secondhand shops, and even a museum.

For adequate apple pie and coffee, any time of the year, stop by **The Country Store,** part of a mercantile that's been open continuously since 1879. The **Enchanted Villa B&B** in the center of town occupies the romantic retreat of English nobleman Victor Sassoon, who allegedly built the two-story house for his mistress in 1941. Don't miss the all-organic **Angels Bakery,** on the east side of Hillsboro, and the nearby **Apple Orchard,** which serves tasty barbecue sandwiches.

Another pseudo ghost town, Kingston, sits astride NM 152 about 9 miles west of Hillsboro. This is said to have been one of the rowdiest mining camps of New Mexico during its heyday more than a century ago, with busy **Kingston Brewery** supplying 22 saloons and 7,000 thirsty residents. The population has dropped to about 25 souls and the primary evidence of past glories is the solid-looking **Percha Valley Bank** building, now a museum, and the old schoolhouse, now a meeting place for something called **The Spit and Whittle Club.** A three-story B&B, the **Black Range Lodge,** has been open here since the 1980s. Its current proprietor is Catherine Wanek, a Hollywood refugee who makes movies on the side.

These villages, along with the Lincoln County ghost town of White Oaks, "are beautiful and magical places," says Albuquerque-based Judith van Gieson, author of seven Neil Hamel mysteries set in New Mexico.

If You Go: Hillsboro is 32 miles west of Truth or Consequences (and I-25) on NM 152. **Apple Festival** information is available from **Sue's Antiques** at **895-5328**. The **Enchanted Villa B&B** is at **895-5686**. To reach **Kingston's Black Range Lodge,** call **895-5652**.

Insider Tip South of Hillsboro about 16 miles on NM 27 is the historic silver mining camp of **Lake Valley,** reduced to a handful of collapsing structures and (since 1994) zero residents. Stop by on the first Saturday of every month and you can join locals for their dance party in the abandoned schoolhouse. The Bureau of Land Management, which administers most real estate in these parts, has designated NM 27 a "scenic byway" between Hillsboro and Nutt, and the lonely vistas are soul stirring. When you get to the latter community—population 2—you'll have your last crack at a cold drink and hot sandwich before taking the I-25 cutoff to Las Cruces or Deming.

Chapter 9

Southeastern New Mexico

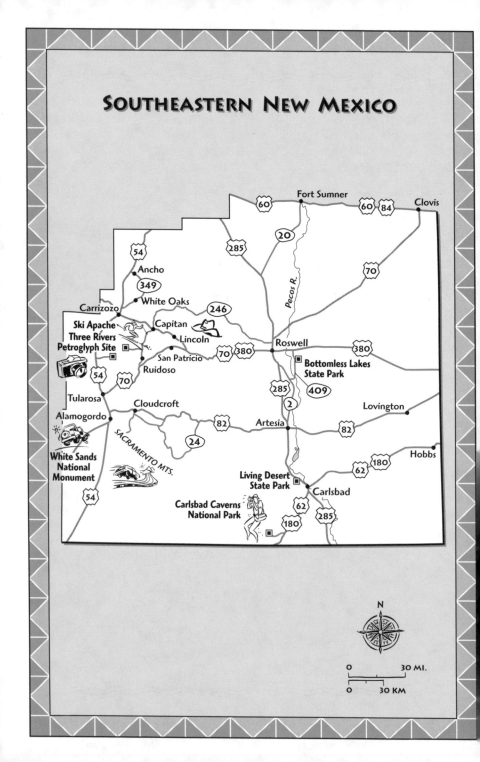

SOUTHEASTERN NEW MEXICO

What's Best about Southeastern New Mexico

Even in a state of dramatic contrasts, the southeastern quadrant of New Mexico is an exceptionally varied place. Head east from Alamogordo to Cloudcroft, for example, and within 20 miles you will pass from the hot Chihuahuan desert to the cool conifers of the Sacramento Mountains. You'll go from a place that gets less than seven inches of rain and a few flakes of snow during an unusually "wet" year to one that receives 30 inches of rain and 70 inches of snow during an unusually "dry" year. You can play golf and tennis in the morning, then ski and ice-skate that same afternoon.

Besides the natural beauty of these lush, pine-covered highlands and arid, sunny lowlands, there is much to experience here. You can gamble at the Mescalero Indian Reservation's flashy casino, or stand in the nineteenth-century courtroom where gunslinger Billy the Kid made a daring escape. At the region's various museums, you can ponder the mysteries of UFOs, the charms of Smokey Bear, and the loveliness of the horse. You can picnic in one of North America's biggest caves, visit the grave of the first primate astronaut, stand in awe before some of the nation's best paintings, and tour a pistachio nut farm.

The people and their cultures of the southeast are equally diverse. You'll meet Hispanos named Smith who can trace their *nuevomexicano* ancestry back for three centuries, and Anglos named Martínez whose forebears fought in the American Revolution. You'll encounter Indians related to Geronimo who drive pickups from Detroit, and squinty-eyed ranchers whose grandfathers ran cattle and whose sons raise ostriches.

For the purposes of this book, southeastern New Mexico is defined as including all or part of Lincoln, Otero, Chaves, Eddy, Lea, Roosevelt, De Baca, and Curry counties. Major towns include Alamogordo, Ruidoso, Cloudcroft, Roswell, Carlsbad, Hobbs, and Portales.

1 *Best* Collection of Amazing Stuff

My House of Old Things was once the Ancho Train Station.

My House of Old Things is just that. It is an enormous building—the defunct Ancho train station, to be exact—crammed ceiling to floor with thousands and thousands of *old things*. Not any old things, mind you, but stuff collected largely by, for, or relating to the pioneering Straley family of central New Mexico. The items are profoundly eclectic, ranging from telegraph keys and railroad memorabilia to matchbox covers and old bottles. You'll find a mint-condition Wurlitzer jukebox, wood-burning kitchen stove, ancient arrowheads, turn-of-the-century toys, and heirloom china. Most of these relics date from 1900 to 1950, when Ancho was a thriving community.

"A tour of My House of Old Things is a nostalgic return to the past for old-timers and an education for anybody under 40, or even 60," says Connie Goldman, coauthor of *Secrets of Becoming a Late Bloomer*, a celebration of the positive aspects of aging. "What amazes me is the museum's large number of everyday household items that have vanished from use, such as wringer washing machines, tube-type radios, iceboxes, coal-heated irons, and horse-drawn wagons."

Most of the collection was assembled by Straley family member Jackie Silvers, postmistress of Ancho for 56 years. The late

Mrs. Silvers's daughter, Sara, now maintains the museum. Sara lives next door with her husband, L. Y. Jackson, and their watchdog, in a shady compound. These three constitute the entire permanent population of Ancho, once home to several hundred people. Many worked in a brick and plaster factory here that is now in ruins.

"I don't accept donations of new items for the museum anymore," sighs Sara Jackson. "I already have too much." Walk in the front door and you'll see what she means.

If You Go: Ancho is 2 miles east of US 54 on CR 349. **My House of Old Things (648-2456)** is 24 miles north of Carizozo and 27 miles south of Corona. Open May 1 through October 15 from 9:00 A.M. to 5:00 P.M. daily. Admission is $2.50 for adults; $1 for children under 12.

2 *Best* Museum in a Bar

Or is it the best bar in a museum?

No matter, just about everything in White Oaks looks like it belongs in a museum anyway. Once the second-largest city in New Mexico, with more than 4,000 people, this gold-mining town is hanging on for dear life with a population of 22 residents.

White Oaks was pretty well spent at the turn of the century, after the easy ore played out and the railroad was re-routed, but some vestiges of its 1880s heyday remain. These include the funky two-room **White Oaks Bar,** where you can sip a cold beer (or a shot of hard stuff) and sometimes hear local bluegrass musicians on Saturday nights or Sunday afternoons. The bar has some old clippings and artifacts on display (it was once the

White Oaks's "No Scum Allowed" Saloon.

newspaper office) as well as an interesting collection of horse tack hanging below the punched-tin ceiling. Jim, who moved from

Michigan a while back to take over the bar and try his hand at prospecting, sells gold flakes he's panned in nearby arroyos. You can play billiards on a couple of dusty pool tables.

Dominating the town is a pair of fine Victorian mansions, referred to by the names of the men who built them. The red brick **Hoyle Castle,** said to be haunted, is a private home; but the **Gumm House,** a 13-room white Victorian on the northeast side of White Oaks, can be toured by prior arrangement. The old schoolhouse (now a community-run museum) is also worth visiting and there are remnants of bars, banks, and bawdy houses. A handful of artists, including a highly-skilled custom saddle-maker, have settled here in recent years and directions to their studios are posted in the center of town at the corner of Pine Street and White Oaks Avenue. No appointments are necessary—simply drop in.

Although now a private residence, the Hoyle Castle is a piece of White Oaks's history and is said to be haunted.

"White Oaks would have unquestionably been a flourishing little metropolis had the leading men not been so greedy," wrote resident historian Ruth Bird-song in a pamphlet about the place. "The El Paso & Northeastern Railroad had plans for the railroad to be built through the town but property owners refused to donate a right of way and priced land so high that the negotiators walked off. A town that started as one of the most promising of all New Mexico sank into oblivion."

On at least one day each year White Oaks regains the equivalent of its early population when thousands of visitors show up for the **Lincoln-White Oaks Pony Express Race.** Riders race each other from Lincoln to the White Oaks Bar, a distance of about 40 miles. This may be the reason the bar is emblazoned with a sign warning, "NO SCUM ALLOWED!" (It used to say, "NO HORSES!" but horses are now apparently preferred to scum.)

If You Go: White Oaks, an official state historic site, is accessible via 8 miles of paved road (NM 349), intersecting US 54 3 miles north of Carizozo. Adventurous travelers may wish to take the scenic dirt road (NM 462) that winds 18 miles south from Ancho via Jicarilla, another old mining village. There is a small gift shop and restaurant in White Oaks, **Birdsong's Crafty Cage,** open 9:00 A.M. to 5:00 P.M. from May to September. The cemetery on the south end of town will interest those intrigued by old-time tombstones in mint condition.

3 *Best* Smokey Bear Memorabilia

The Smokey Bear Museum is also the final resting place of the famous black bear.

Capitán is home to the **Smokey Bear Museum, Smokey Bear Historical State Park, Smokey Bear Motel,** and **Smokey Bear Boulevard.** It is also the dear fellow's last resting place.

Yes, there really was a Smokey Bear. (The guardians of his story are quick to point out that the bruin's correct name is *not* Smokey *the* Bear.) The first Smokey was a charred, orphaned cub rescued by fire-fighters in 1950 after a dangerous wildfire swept through nearby wilderness. This black bear became a living symbol of the U.S. Forest Service's fire prevention campaign and spent most of his days waving to school children at the National Zoo in Washington, D.C.

Smokey died in 1976 and was buried on the grounds of the state park here. The landscaping in the courtyard around the original Smokey's grave is noteworthy because it demonstrates through native plants how dramatically different the climate zones of New Mexico are, ranging from desert cacti to the conifers of the state's highest mountains.

"It's the perfect resting place for a conservation-minded bear," says Kent DeVore, a local wildlife biologist.

The park's museum screens an unusually informative and entertaining film about Smokey on request (both children and adults will enjoy it), and there is a well-curated exhibit with all sorts of odd tidbits, including Mr. Bear's wry obituary in the *Washington Post* and lyrics to all four verses of the "Smokey Bear" song.

Next door is a log-cabin gift shop, built in 1960 by a local women's club and now maintained by the Capitán Chamber of Commerce. Trivia is raised to new heights here—you can buy everything from "official" Smokey Bear ash trays and pencils to Smokey dolls and Frisbees.

If You Go: The **state park (354-2748),** gravesite, and museum gift shop are adjacent to one another in downtown Capitán (165 miles southeast of Albuquerque) on US 380 near the intersection of NM 48. There are picnic facilities on the premises but no camping. On the Fourth of July, Capitán residents celebrate the **Smokey Bear Stampede,** complete with a parade, barbecue, rodeo, fun run, Western dance, and, naturally, commemoration of the life and good works of Smokey Bear. The **Lincoln County Fair** is held here every second week of August. State park admission is 25¢.

4 *Best* Gourmet Meal in Capitán

The Hotel Chango, though not a hotel, offers some of the best international cuisine in the state.

Don't be misled, **Hotel Chango** is not a hotel. It's the name of its owner's now deceased pet cat (slang for "monkey" in Spanish). It's also a tiny restaurant that serves some of the best international cuisine in New Mexico, despite the curious fact that it is tucked away in the Smokey Bear—obsessed village of Capitán.

Jerrold Flores is the only one who can explain what this gem of an eatery is doing here, and he's the sort of fellow who'll shrug his head at such a question and then offer another helping of polenta. Or perhaps expound upon the museum-quality art collection that graces the restaurant's crowded rooms. Flores, a native of nearby Fort Stanton, is Chango's mercurial owner and artist in residence. He oversees an evolving menu and welcomes dinner guests Tuesday through Saturday nights. During the off times, Jerrold makes paintings and sculpture, or travels around the world.

"At least that's what I'd like to be doing," laughs Flores, whose home and studio is next door. "Running a restaurant is pretty much a full-time job for me."

The job pays off for Hotel Chango's lucky customers.

"It was orgasmic," swooned *El Paso Times* food critic Pat Barker, describing her first meal there in 1992 (and the author of this book agrees). "Food is love, and Jerrold Flores is a lover ... Hotel Chango was a consummate dining experience."

Barker's enthusiasm is seconded by Albuquerque-based food writer Sally Moore. "The best eating I've had in New Mexico," Moore declares. "Both the food and presentation are remarkable."

Expect stylish, creative dishes, such as poached salmon with smoked chiles and pork tenderloin in chipotle orange sauce. Desserts, wines, and appetizers are also excellent.

If You Go: Full of treasures from Guatemala and the Southwest, **Hotel Chango (354-4213)** is situated at the intersection of US 380 and NM 48. Prices are moderately expensive, with full wine service. Summer hours are from 5:00 P.M. "until closing." Reservations advised.

5 *Best* Billy the Kid Obsession

To observe that **Lincoln** dwells on its past is like saying that Hollywood is preoccupied with show biz. Those who say this now bucolic village peaked a century ago are not exaggerating. You can reasonably argue that the crest came more than 115 years ago, when the locally famous Lincoln County War turned the place into a hotbed of turmoil and intrigue.

The local populace divided into feuding factions (Tunstall/McSween vs. Murphy/Dolan) during the bloody summer of 1878. William "Billy the Kid" Bonney—a young cowboy who went on a shooting spree to avenge the death of his boss, rancher John

Tunstall—was hunted down and killed by Sheriff Pat Garrett. The Kid met his end not in Lincoln, but 140 miles away in Fort Sumner, at the home of millionaire Lucien Bonaparte Maxwell. Billy's body lies in a cemetery there, marked by a gravestone that is fenced off to thwart vandals.

The Old County Courthouse of Lincoln is an authentic example of territorial New Mexican architecture.

The entire four-block-long village of Lincoln is a state and national historic monument overseen by the Museum of New Mexico. Many of the original buildings, including the county courthouse and Tunstall's store, are in remarkably good condition and open to the public. About one-third of the property in town is owned by the Lincoln County Historical Trust or the State of New Mexico, with the balance in the hands of private citizens who have generally done an excellent job of maintaining its 1880s look. Many residents also volunteer as hosts and hostesses at the town's many museums. Bolstered by a strict architectural code, the resulting ambiance is not unlike Virginia's colonial Williamsburg.

"The various restored homes and businesses here are among the best examples of territorial architecture in New Mexico," says John Boylan, an architectural historian who helped develop **Lincoln Historical Monument** during the 1950s and 1960s. "I recommend particularly a visit to the **Old Courthouse,** which is full of period furniture, artifacts, and photos."

If You Go: Lincoln is on US 380, 12 miles east of Capitán and 10 miles west of Hondo. It's 195 miles southeast of Albuquerque and 35 miles northeast of Ruidoso. Admission to the **Historical Center** is $4.50 (children under 17 free), open 9:00 A.M. to 5:00 P.M. Despite Lincoln's notoriety, food and lodging is limited (and kitschy gift shops are nonexistent). There are a few tasteful galleries and specialty stores, however. Besides the **Casa de Patrón,** described below, rooms are available at the **Ellis Store B&B (653-4609)** and sometimes at the **Wortley Hotel (653-4300)**. Snacks and drinks are available, but there are no service stations or groceries. For information, contact the **Lincoln County Heritage Trust** at **653-4025**. The first weekend in August is set aside for **Old Lincoln Days**, with a parade, rodeo, barbecue, and lectures by Billy the Kid buffs.

Insider Tip The best way to see things is on a self-guided walking tour, picking up an annotated map at the **Historical Center and Museum.** The map provides a detailed history of the 39 historic structures in the center of Lincoln. A slide show at the center provides a helpful introduction, including details about a contingent of Buffalo Soldiers that was sent to keep the peace after the Lincoln County War. There are also artifacts relating to early Hispano and Indian inhabitants, who made this their home long before whites arrived in the mid–1800s. A fascinating remnant of the Spanish Colonial era is the *torreón*, a stone tower once used to shelter townsfolk from marauders. Also noteworthy is the **San Juan Mission,** a restored church built in 1888.

6 *Best* B&B Billy the Kid Slept In

When Texas engineer Jerry Jordan and his wife, Cleis, fled the Houston rat race a few years ago, Lincoln is where they unwound. And the cozy **Casa de Patrón** is what they wound up creating. It's a charming adobe (on the National Register of Historic Buildings) that was once home to Juan Patrón, a storekeeper and the youngest House Speaker in the territorial legislature. He hosted Billy the Kid as an overnight guest several times—during New Mexico's early days it was customary for families to open their homes to weary travelers, potential outlaws included—and in 1879 Billy escaped from detention here. The house is shaded and comfortable, full of traditional New Mexican stylings (vigas and tile work) as well as antique Victorian furniture.

Casa de Patrón has three guest rooms in the old house, two *casitas* (small adobe homes), and two rooms in a separate building.

Continental breakfasts are offered in the casitas, gourmet breakfasts for other guests are served in the main house. An elegant and delicious evening meal is served by prior arrangement No-

Billy the Kid slept here—The Casa de Patrón and owner Jerry Jordan.

vember through May (registered guests only). With prompting and good humor, the Jordans will entertain their dinner guests with live keyboard music and song. Not to be missed is their collection of more than 100 old washboards and fragrant soap bars (made on the premises).

"This place is a real treat," says Linda Rodolitz, a former restaurant critic. "What makes it all work is the fact that the Jordans love what they do. Their attention to beauty and detail really shows."

If You Go: For information, call **653-4676** or write **Box 27, Lincoln, NM 88338. Casa de Patrón** is located on **Main Street (US 380)** in the heart of Lincoln. The best restaurant options include the Italian bistro **La Bella,** in nearby Ruidoso, and the previously mentioned **Hotel Chango** in Capitán.

7 *Best* Desert Petroglyphs

More than 20,000 individual Indian rock carvings have been counted at **Three Rivers Petroglyph Site,** located next to a partially excavated Jornado Mogollon village at the base of the Sacramento Mountains north of Alamogordo. Experts believe the petroglyphs were made more than a thousand years ago by tribal people who roamed the Tularosa Basin.

"What is especially unusual about the carvings found at Three Rivers is the large number of geometric designs found here, along with the more commonplace human and animal figures," says archaeologist and Three Rivers fan T. J. Fitch. "No one knows the exact meaning of these exotic designs, some of which are very intricate and artistic. My feeling is that these were created simply as art objects, for the sheer pleasure of both the creator and viewer."

Some of the more than 5,000 drawings here show game animals, including antelope and turkey, while many of the abstract drawings are believed to have religious meaning.

If You Go: The **Three Rivers Petroglyph Site** is located on public land and includes a shaded picnic area. The petroglyphs are strewn over several rocky hillsides that become very hot during the summer months. Allow at least an hour for the 0.5-mile walk along a lonely ridge top where the petroglyphs are located. Turn east from US 54 at the Three Rivers turnoff, 17 miles north of Tularosa (28 miles south of Carizozo), and go 5 miles to the petroglyphs. Another 8 miles up the canyon is the **Three Rivers Camping Area,** surrounded by trees and watered by a cool spring.

8 *Best* Pistachio Orchard

For the uninitiated, pistachio nuts are tasty, high-fiber, cholesterol-free snacks that originated in the Persian Gulf countries but are now grown in arid regions of the Southwest. The nuts are low in saturated fat, high in carbohydrates, and provide a good nutritional balance.

"These pistachios are the best," concludes photographer Merilyn Brown, who has roamed the back roads of New Mexico for more than a dozen years. "I also like driving NM 54 north of here, toward Carizozo. There are vast views of open land and distant mountains, with almost no traffic."

Orchard tours are offered weekdays at **Eagle Pistachio Ranch** near Alamogordo. The Schweers family compound contains New Mexico's first and largest groves of pistachio nut trees, first planted in 1972. They sell pistachios (under the "Heart of the Desert" label) that are raw, roasted, salted, shelled, or seasoned with red or green chile.

If You Go: Open daily from 9:00 A.M. to 6:00 P.M., **Eagle Ranch** is 4 miles north of Alamogordo on NM 54/70 North. Information: **800-432-0999.** Tours are given at 1:30 P.M. daily. You'll visit the orchards, processing center, and Eagle's gift shop, where nuts (as well as Indian jewelry and T-shirts) can be purchased. Other orchards in the area are open to tourists, but Eagle offers the best tours and facilities.

9 *Best* Space Museum by a Fat Cottonwood

Founded in 1898 as a railroad hub for the nearby Sacramento Mountains lumber industry, Alamogordo ("fat cottonwood") is now a space-age city with an economy largely dependent on nearby Holloman Air Force Base and the White Sands Missile Range. You can experience some of the technological marvels advanced at these two facilities by visiting the **International Space Museum and Hall of Fame,** which displays satellites, astronauts' capsules, rocket engines, and many devices used in space exploration. There's even a "simulated Mars room" where you can pretend you're visiting the red planet, and the Space Station 2001, with visitor-operated controls. Particularly worth seeing is the **Clyde W. Tombaugh Space Theater** next door, which offers planetarium programs, laser light shows, and big-screen, 180-degree OMNIMAX movies (the latter requires a separate fee of $2.75, children $1.25).

"I love bringing people here, especially kids," says geologist Harrison "Jack" Schmitt, former U.S. Senator from New Mexico—now an Albuquerque-based consultant—and one of only 12 astronauts who have walked on the moon. "You come away with a very realistic picture of what our space program is all about, how it's advanced our level of knowledge in so many ways—and how New Mexico has played a vital part."

If You Go: Alamogordo is four hours from Albuquerque and 75 minutes from Las Cruces. The five-story **International Space Museum and Hall of Fame (800-545-4021)** is on **Scenic Drive at Indian Wells Road,** a short distance from US 70. Admission is $2.25 for adults (seniors half price), $1.75 for children; open daily except Christmas from 9:00 A.M. to 5:00 P.M. (until 6:00 P.M. in summer). The theater, which has a separate entrance and screens movies six times a day, is also open at night. Gift shops in both buildings are best bets for science-oriented items. The best meals in town are served at **Margo's,** a cozy Mexican restaurant at **501 First Street.**

10 Best Place to Experience the Full Moon

Few sights are more eerily spectacular than watching the enormous white disc rise slowly into the desert sky from behind the snow-capped Sacramento Mountains, while the golden sun simultaneously sinks behind the San Andres range to the west.

"This is the perfect place to go for romance," declares landscape photographer Debbie Carley, who has also modeled in the gypsum dunes of **White Sands National Monument,** where this magnificence unfolds. "There's something about the soft curves of the sand and the gentle glow of the moon that is very mysterious and sensuous."

The monument, southwest of Alamogordo, is only open to non-campers during nighttime hours when there is a full moon. Campers are welcome any time and visitors can walk by day through snow-white dunes (some 60 feet high) and cactus-studded depressions that undulate for miles in every direction. Plants and animals have developed amazing adaptations to this harsh environment and a moonlit night is the best time to observe them.

The dunes are formed when spring winds carry gypsum particles from the dry bed of Lake Lucero, southwest of the park, and deposit them in wave-like patterns over the broad Tularosa Valley. (Three-hour-long auto caravans to this unique source of the white sand take place about nine times a year, by reservation only.) At 300 square miles, this is the largest gypsum dune complex in the world, easily seen from orbiting spacecraft.

If You Go: **White Sands National Monument (479-6124)** is on US 70/82, about 15 miles southwest of Alamogordo. Open 8:00 A.M. to

9:00 P.M. Memorial Day through Labor Day, 8:00 A.M. to sunset the rest of the year, for a $4 admission fee. The park is open to non-campers until after midnight on full moon nights (including the actual evening of the full moon and one day on either side; check for exact dates) June through October. Rangers present a special evening program on these occasions.

Insider Tip White Sands is the best place in New Mexico to see an **oryx**. These elk-sized African antelope were transplanted in the 1970s at the behest of big-game hunters anxious to bag a trophy. Conditions were so ideal that there are now hundreds of oryx, distinguished by their long, sharp horns and white-on-black stripes. If you see one, stay in your car or keep your distance: these animals are notoriously aggressive.

11 *Best* Haunted Hotel

Where's Rebecca?

Those who work (or stay) in **The Lodge at Cloudcroft,** in the mountains east of Alamogordo, swear that she's pacing the floors, flitting through the tower, stumbling through the kitchen, and otherwise causing a nuisance at inopportune moments.

Rebecca is the ghost of a flirtatious, red-haired hotel chambermaid whose restless temperament is said to derive from her murder in the 1930s at the hand of a jealous lover. But the presence of a relatively benign ghost hasn't deterred the rich and famous from spending the night here. Judy Garland, Pancho Villa, and Clark Gable are among the many celebrity guests who've dented pillows at The Lodge since it opened in 1899.

A registered historic landmark, the Victorian-style hotel has 47 rooms, each lovingly restored and furnished with turn-of-the-century antiques. The high-backed beds are covered in down quilts that invite snuggling. One of The Lodge's most interesting features is its copper-domed observatory, located four flights above the lobby and accessible only by a single brass skeleton key. From the tower's windows, you can see hundreds of square miles of verdant fir and pine forest. Ask at the front desk about scheduled tours.

"This is New Mexico's best-kept secret," declares Beth Clay, a freelance travel writer for *Southwest Profile* and other regional magazines. "The entire atmosphere of The Lodge is reminiscent of a large party in a private home."

The Lodge restaurant—called **Rebecca's,** of course—invites romance and treats diners to an exquisite meal, soothing piano music, and a breathtaking view of the Tularosa Basin below as well as the cozy alpine village of Cloudcroft, perched at an elevation of 9,200 feet.

In addition to the ghost of a flirtatious chambermaid, The Lodge houses a fine restaurant and offers Victorian-style lodging—just ask Rebecca.

If You Go: Cloudcroft is 18 miles east of Alamogordo on US 82, and about 45 miles south of Ruidoso via US 70 and NM 244. Reservations are advised for both **The Lodge's** hotel and restaurant: call **800-395-6343.** Prices are moderate, varying by season. The Lodge is about 100 yards off NM 82 at 1 Corona Place. The **Cloudcroft Chamber of Commerce** dispenses information at **682-2733.**

Insider Tip Once the terminus of a narrow-gauge lumber railroad (The Lodge was originally a railroad-built resort), Cloudcroft boasts a golf course (said to be the highest-altitude course in the United States), Nordic ski trails, art galleries, and a historical museum that highlights the bygone railroad era. Other attractions include the **Cloud-Climbing Rail Trail** (a hiking trail that stretches from Alamogordo through La Luz and Cloudcroft to Sunspot), snowmobiling, outdoor ice-skating, and skiing at the southernmost ski facility in the United States (referred to both as **Ski Cloudcroft** and **Snow Canyon**). Summer highlights include swimming, camping, horseback riding, mountain biking, fishing, as well as annual bluegrass music and "Western roundup" festivals.

Besides The Lodge, which operates two annexes (**The Retreat** and **The Pavilion**), there are plenty of alternative hotels, motels, and campgrounds in the Cloudcroft area. **National Forest Service** info: **682-2551.**

12 *Best* Solar Observatory

Sunspot, as you might expect, is one of the best places to see the sun. Don't expect to see a lot of people in this minuscule New Mexico community, however. Most of the 70 or so residents spend their time indoors, examining things like solar winds, coronas, and magnetic storms. All are features of our nearest neighborhood star—a medium-sized sphere we call the sun—that's under near-constant surveillance from a promontory in the Sacramento Mountains, 18 miles south of Cloudcroft.

"This is one of the world's largest solar observation centers," explained the late Lucy White, who lived in Sunspot for several years with her astronomer husband. "Several large telescopes are in virtual 'round-the-clock use."

Well-marked signs direct visitors to the observatory compound, where self-guided tours begin at a central parking lot and picnic area. Several solar telescopes can be viewed during the tour, including the original one: housed in a Sears mail-order barn. The largest telescope extends from 20 stories underground to 13 stories above. A video screen allows visitors to see what scientists are focusing on, and there is a collection of impressive photos taken at the site. A lookout point on the escarpment of Sacramento Peak provides an awesome view.

If You Go: The **National Solar Observatory (434-7000)** is reached via NM 130 and NM 6563 from Cloudcroft. Open daily from 8:00 A.M. to 5:00 P.M., with guided tours at 2:00 P.M. Saturdays from May to October. There are no admission fees and no services beyond a soda machine and restrooms. Picnic tables are near the visitors' center.

Insider Tip About 0.25 mile east of the solar observation site on NM 6563 is **Apache Point Observatory,** a cluster of four telescopes used to study the night sky. Privately operated by a consortium of research institutes and universities, the complex uses state-of-the-art technologies to collect data on stars, galaxies, quasars, and other astronomical features. The telescopes are often operated by remote control, with data relayed to distant research centers via satellite. Apache Point was chosen because of its clean air and the absence of light pollution from large cities. A relative absence of strong winds allows images to be sharp and clear. A sign on the spur road leading into Apache Point indicates whether visitors can be accommodated (this varies, depending on what kind of study is underway). Information: **437-6822.**

13 *Best* Enclosed Skiers' Gondola

Ski Apache is operated by the Mescalero Apache tribe on the slopes of its sacred peak—an extinct 12,003-foot volcano called Sierra Blanca—in the Sacramento Mountains. This modern facility not only boasts New Mexico's only enclosed gondola, but also the largest uphill lift capacity in the state. The Mescaleros have groomed 52 runs and trails (many rated advanced) on "Old Baldy" and operate eight chairlifts. Nearby is a ski rental shop, bar, restaurant and a hotel.

"It's hard to beat the view at Ski Apache," says Dan Gibson, a New Mexico native and syndicated outdoor sports columnist. "From Sierra Blanca you look down into the pink, tan, and cream-colored landscape of White Sands, more than 7,000 vertical feet below." Gibson notes that Ski Apache receives an average of 190 inches of snow each winter and there are runs for every ability level.

The best place in New Mexico to play the odds may very well be the nearby **Casino Apache,** which offers poker, lotto, eight-way, and other video gaming on the Mescalero Apache Indian

Reservation about 3.5 miles southwest of Ruidoso. The enterprise is in the conference center of the **Inn of the Mountain Gods,** a sprawling resort perched beside man-made Lake Mescalero. The resort itself is pricey and rather sterile, with such amenities as tennis, skeet shooting, and golf. Both the casino and the resort are owned and operated by the Mescalero Apache, although there is precious little commemoration of the tribe and its culture on display.

If your visit coincides with the July 4th holiday, you can attend the **Mescalero Apache Ceremonial and Rodeo,** which includes the colorful Dance of the Apache Maidens, bareback riding, barrel racing, traditional foods, and a cross-country run. During this or other stays, be sure to check out the **Apache Cultural Center** in the village of Mescalero for an informative exhibition of the tribe's history and art.

If You Go: **Ski Apache** is reached by taking NM 48 to the village of Alto, a few miles north of Ruidoso, then west about 9 miles on NM 532. Contact **257-9001** for information and ski conditions. No matter what the season, the **Mescalero Apache Reservation (800-545-9011)** contains some of the prettiest scenery in the state. The tribe's lands cut across a wide, lush swath of the Sacramento Mountains from Ruidoso nearly all the way to Cloudcroft.

14 *Best* Place to See Hurd/Wyeth Family Art

The Hurd-LaRinconada Gallery in San Patricio.

San Patricio is one of the few old Hispano villages in southern New Mexico that has retained its ambiance and culture. Located in the fertile Río Hondo Valley and dominated by fruit orchards and cattle ranches, San Patricio has attracted many writers and artists over the years. Most notable are the Hurd and Wyeth families, a product of the marriage of painters Peter Hurd and Henriette Wyeth. Hurd died some years ago, but his widow and children still live in the area, and their beloved Sentinel Ranch rents adobe "guest homes" to overnight visitors. These lovely *casitas* require a two-night minimum and are fully furnished.

A must-see in San Patricio is the **Hurd-LaRinconada Gallery,** a beautifully designed building that houses an extensive collection of Hurd-Wyeth family art, including many works by patriarch Peter Hurd. Inexpensive prints are on sale and photocopies of the family genealogy help sort out who's who. In front of the gallery is a polo field where local equestrians play every weekend through summer and fall.

Another San Patricio attraction is **Fort Meigs,** the antique-filled home of Johnny Meigs, an artist and art collector whose rambling estate is across the arroyo from the Hurd-LaRinconada Gallery. During a colorful career that has taken him around the world many times, Meigs has accumulated hundreds of paintings, graphics, drawings, engravings, furniture, ceramics, Asian artifacts, scrolls, and books. Many of

Once the home of artist and art collector Johnny Miegs, Fort Meigs is now home to an extensive collection of art, antiques, and books.

these were acquired by the Museum of New Mexico, but some of the finest items are still on display in a gallery that overlooks the Río Hondo. Its gardens are so lovely that this has become a popular site for outdoor weddings.

"San Patricio wouldn't be nearly so interesting without Johnny Meigs, Peter Hurd, and Henriette Wyeth," declares Lucie Yeaman, a retired local apple rancher who has managed to get acquainted with all three during her 90-plus years. "They really captured the spirit of the place, which is so very special."

If You Go: For information on the **Hurd-LaRinconada Gallery** or **Sentinel Ranch Casitas,** call **800-658-6912;** for **Fort Meigs** call

653-4320. To reach any of these, follow the signs a short distance south from US 70.

Insider Tip

There's a small restaurant and grocery in San Patricio, along with summer fruit stands, but the hungry traveler is better off driving a few miles east on US 70 to Tinnie, where the **Silver Dollar Restaurant and Lounge** serves up fine food and drink in an old general store that's been converted into a charming Victorian-style roadhouse. During the 1970s, Johnny Meigs helped renovate the structure, most recently a post office and mercantile. The restaurant and bar are decorated with rare antiques and oil paintings. Check out the ornate European music box of the 1880s which still plays tunes of the last century. From May through September, live concert music floats over the veranda and gardens. The Silver Dollar **(653-4425)** is open for dinner Wednesday through Sunday and lunch on weekends.

15 *Best* Museums for UFO Buffs

When E.T. calls home, he finds a phone booth in New Mexico. It's said that there have been more sightings of unidentified flying objects (UFOs) recorded here than anywhere else. Perhaps it has something to do with the state's bustling secret military activity? Maybe extraterrestrials are attracted by the state's rich deposits of uranium, molybdenum, and dinosaur bones? Could it be that Chaco Canyon was once inhabited by beings from another planet?

A visit to the nonprofit **International UFO (Unidentified Flying Object) Museum and Research Center** in Roswell won't answer any of these questions definitively and will probably prompt even more. For example, was that really a crashed spacecraft that a Lincoln County rancher found on a June day in 1947? Did a flying saucer crash-land on New Mexico's San Agustín Plain later that same year?

"Many books have been written about 'the Roswell incident,'" says Clive Reed, president of the American UFO Society. "I'm convinced that aliens really did touch down on a New Mexico cattle ranch and that our government retrieved some of these creatures."

The government officially dismisses such reports—the Army says the flying saucer was a weather balloon—but hundreds of New Mexicans disagree. The museum's gift shop sells UFO-related coffee mugs, postcards, books, and T-shirts. You can even buy replicas of the wreckage northwest of Roswell that allegedly included blue-tinged metal covered with oddball hieroglyphics.

"We're trying to present an honest picture," explains Walter Haut, president of the International UFO Museum. "We're making available all the materials that exist, so that the individual can make up his or her own mind." To that end, the museum maintains an extensive archive and exhibit space.

A separate facility, **The UFO Enigma Museum,** was opened in 1992 to focus primarily on the "Roswell Incident" of 1947 and to display UFO photos from around the world.

If You Go: The **International UFO Museum (625-9495)** is open daily from 1:00 to 5:00 P.M., at **400-402 North Main.** Admission is free. The **Enigma Museum (347-2275)** is at **6108 South Main,** open from 10:00 A.M. to 5:00 P.M. daily (except Sunday). The **Roswell Inn (623-4920)** at **1815 North Main** "is by far the favorite breakfast place for locals," says Marilyn Watson, a Roswell painter and food critic. "My husband Don likes the green chile stew." The best lunch-time ambiance is found at the **Pecos Rose Tearoom (625-9256),** in an 1885 Victorian home at **709 North Main.** Inquire about once-a-week gourmet dinners. Natural attractions include the **Mescalero Sand Dunes** (40 miles east), **Bottomless Lakes State Park** (about 15 miles east), and **Bitter Lake National Wildlife Refuge** (5 miles northeast).

Insider Tip For a different perspective on space travel, stop by the **Roswell Museum, Planetarium, and Art Center** for a peek at the recreated testing laboratory of scientist Dr. Robert Goddard. Engines and assemblies of the world's first liquid-fuel rockets are on display here (among paintings by Peter Hurd and Georgia O'Keeffe).

"Goddard's tests of rockets near Roswell in the 1930s and Wernher von Braun's rocket research for the U.S.

Army near White Sands after World War II began the modern space age," says former astronaut Harrison Schmitt. "Their work led directly to the huge Saturn V rockets used by me and my Apollo colleagues to explore the moon."

The Roswell Museum, Planetarium, and Art Center **(624-6744)** is at **100 West 11th Street.** Admission is free and hours are 9:00 A.M. to 5:00 P.M., Monday through Saturday, 1:00 to 5:00 P.M. Sundays and holidays.

16 *Best* Holes in the Ground

Of New Mexico's largest and most spectacular cave, adventurer Tim Cahill proclaimed in the March 1991 issue of *National Geographic* that "No one can say how much of this extraordinary underground wilderness there is to explore, or what wonders remain to be found."

Indeed, only a tiny fraction of **Lechuguilla Cave** has been inventoried and its passages are still unfolding. The site is not nearly as well known to the general public as the neighboring **Carlsbad Caverns** complex, but spelunkers (cave explorers) and scientists from around the world consider it the best of the best. Why? Because it is believed to be America's deepest cave (at 1,567 feet) and one of its most pristine. Unseen by humans until 1986, a series of expeditions sponsored by the National Geographic Society has confirmed 89 miles of passages, with no end in sight. Some microbes and fossils in the cave date back millions of years, to the days when this part of New Mexico was covered by a vast inland sea.

In order to preserve its wild qualities, Lechuguilla is not open to uninvited visitors and has been designated an underground wilderness by the government.

Carlsbad, meanwhile, still is New Mexico's best cave for the casual visitor. Formed over the past 250 million years by water and acids seeping through prehistoric limestone, the cavern includes at least 30 miles of passages. The **Big Room,** which boasts a restaurant, lavatories, and gift shop, is bigger than 14 football fields and 25 stories tall, making it the largest known underground chamber in the United States.

Besides incredible stalagmites and stalactites, Carlsbad is home from May through October to hundreds of thousands of Mexican free-tail bats, which use this as a breeding den. The sight of them streaming en masse out of the main entrance at sunset is awesome. Sadly, there were once millions more bats here, but human activity has displaced most of them.

Carlsbad Caverns National Park encompasses 47,000 acres and is open year-round. There are regularly scheduled tours of the main cave—ranging from easy to strenuous—and an elevator provides easy access for those who don't wish to make the steep climb into the cave on foot.

The undeveloped **Slaughter Canyon Cave** (formerly called The New Cave) is 23 miles from the main Carlsbad cavern and New Mexico's best cave for the adventurous. It may be visited twice daily during the summer (Memorial Day through Labor Day) and on weekends the rest of the year. Getting to the entrance requires a strenuous 0.5-mile uphill hike through desert country once inhabited by the Guadalupe Indians, as evidenced by the beautiful rock drawings seen en route. Ranger-guided lantern tours of the Slaughter Canyon Cave last about 90 minutes, cost $8, and day-ahead reservations are required (no children under age six allowed). Bring a flashlight, hiking shoes, and water.

If You Go: **Carlsbad Caverns National Park** is 26 miles southwest of the city of Carlsbad. Take US 62/180 south to White's City, then west on NM 7. Admission fees to the park and cavern vary depending on your vehicle and length of stay. Information and reservations: **785-2232**. Temperatures at the park are hot above ground during the summer but uniformly cool (56°F) down below: bring a long-sleeve shirt or light jacket as well as sturdy shoes. Slaughter Canyon Cave is reached via a gravel road from US 62-180, 5 miles southwest of White's City. There's no campground at the park; the nearest hotels and motels are in White's City and Carlsbad. Camping is available in **Guadalupe Mountains National Park,** across the border in Texas. Carlsbad's other worthwhile attractions include the **Living Desert Museum and Zoo State Park** and, from Thanksgiving through December 25, a fanciful display of holiday lights along scenic Lake Carlsbad that are viewed from aboard pontoon boats under the auspices of the **Carlsbad Chamber of Commerce (887-6516)**.

Insider Tip There are two self-guided tours of Carlsbad Cavern, one departing from the main natural entrance and the other from the elevator inside the visitors' center.

Rangers lead several highly recommended tours each week to remote areas of **Carlsbad Cavern** and nearby **Spider Cave.** These last from one to four hours, cost $12, and you should sign up in advance. You must be physically fit and over age 16 to participate. Also recommended is the daily ranger-led King's Palace Tour ($5). Air-conditioned kennels are available to travelers with pets.

Index

A

B

balloning, 59, 87–88, 161
Bandalier National Monument, 44–45
Bandera Volcano and Ice Cave, 135–136
Bareiss, Philip, 60–62
Barker, Pat, 195
baseball, 120
   Connie Mack World Series Baseball Tournament, 120
Bataan Death March, 30
Begel, Deborah, 73
Benally, Eve, 162
Best of the Best, 1–17
Billy the Kid (William Bonney), 28, 161–163, 189, 194–198
Bingham, 113
Birdsong, Ruth, 192
Bistí Badland, 118, 123–124
Blue Hole, 160–161
Bosland, Paul W., 10
Bosque del Apache National Wildlife Refuge, 109–111
Bosque Redondo, 162
Boylan, John, 196
Brooker, Valerie, 129–130
Brown, Merilyn, 145, 199

C

Caballo Lake, 184
Cabeza de Vaca, Álvar Núñez, 71
Cabot, Denise, 72
Cadena, Rita, 160
Cahill, Tom, 210
camping, 103, 107, 124, 126, 137, 148, 158–160, 174, 176, 199, 201, 203–204, 211
Capitán, 16, 193–195, 198
Caprock Amphitheater, 161
Capulín Volcano National Monument, 158–159
Carizozo, 191, 199
Carlsbad, 211–212
Carlsbad Caverns National Park, 210–212
Carson, Kit, 158
Castellano, Pedro, 112
Cather, Willa, 34
Cerrillos, 101
Cerro, 69
Chaco Canyon, 124–126
Chama, 16, 70–71
Chappell, Mike, 171
Chávez, Manuela and Pablo, 101–102
children's activities, 15–17, 28–30
chile, 10–12, 111–112, 168–169
Chile Institute, 11
Chimayó, 42–44
   El Santuario de Chimayó, 42–43
churches, 23–24, 71, 106–107, 131, 133, 145, 150, 197
Cimarron, 156–158
City of Rocks State Park, 173–174
Clay, Beth, 203
Cleveland Roller Mill, 151–152
climate, 14–15
Cloudcroft, 189, 202–204
Clovis, 161
Coggan, Catherine, 29
Collins, Jennifer, 95

About the Author

*R*ichard Mahler is a journalist, author, and photographer who specializes in travel writing, among many other subjects. He is a published author of five books and has been a freelance reporter for National Public Radio since 1973 and for the *Los Angeles Times* since 1979. He has written thousands of articles for more than 100 magazines and newspapers, including the *New Mexican*, *New Mexico* magazine, and *Santa Fean* magazine. A longtime resident of New Mexico, Mahler lives in Santa Fe.

Notes